Messengers Of Hope

by
CAROL W. PARRISH-HARRA

Published by:
NEW AGE PRESS
P.O. Box 1216
Black Mountain, NC 28711

ISBN 0-87613-079-1

Cover by Frederick Bennett Green

Rev. Carol W. Parrish-Harra
Light of Christ Community Church
P.O. Box 1274
Tahlequah, Oklahoma 74465

Dedicated to those
who have eyes with which to see
and
ears with which to hear

The author wants to acknowledge the many who helped make this book possible. Certainly, I wish to acknowledge Ruth Montgomery and the push she game me to tell my story, to Rusty Petters who figured it out, and to Charles who has the courage it takes to participate in my life. I thank my editor, Bethany Link for the polish she gives my words and appreciation to Caroline Bremer and Judith Katz for the many hours of detailed work and day to day support that I needed.

Messengers Of Hope

"If you are a disciple of the Master, it is up to you to illumine the earth. You do not have to groan over everything the world lacks; you are there to bring it what it needs . . . there, where reigns hatred, malice and discord, you will put Love, Pardon and Peace. For lying you will bring truth; for despair, hope; for doubt, faith; where there is sadness, you will give joy. If you are, in the smallest degree, the servant of God, all these virtues of Light you will carry with you . . . do not be frightened by a mission so vast! It is not really you who are charged with the fulfillment of it. You are only the Torch-bearer. The fire, even if it burns within you, even when it burns you, is never lit by you. It uses you as it uses the oil of the lamp. You hold it, feed it, carry it around; but it is the fire that works, that gives the light to the world, and to yourself at the same time . . . do not be the clogged lantern that chokes and smothers the Light; the lamp, timid, or ashamed, hidden under a bushel; flame up and shine before men; lift high the fire of God."

Phillippe Vernier
(After World War II)

TABLE OF CONTENTS

Foreward

by Kenneth Ring, Ph.D.

When the author of this book called me to request that I contribute a foreward, I was initially very flattered to be asked. But when she went on to inform me that her book dealt with her life as a "Walk-in," shudders of second thoughts quickly arose in my mind and I began to wonder whether I should retract my consent before it was too late.

I was familiar with Ruth Montgomery's concept of a "Walk-in"—supposedly a highly developed spiritual entity who, usually during a spiritual or near-death crisis, enters into and takes over the functioning of a human being who no longer wishes to live—from reading her book, *Strangers Among Us,* but as a scientist, I found it too *outre* to put much credence in. I also knew that Carol Parrish-Harra had been specifically identified by Ruth Montgomery in her latest book, *Threshold to Tomorrow,* as a "Walk-in" and though I have to admit that I found many of Mrs. Montgomery's case histories in that book to be utterly fascinating, I still had difficulty swallowing her "Walk-in" interpretation of her material. I didn't even like the term she chose; it smacked, I thought, of tabloid journalism. I am just a snob about such things, I suppose. Nevertheless, I had to concede that, whatever the explanation of the phenomenon Ruth Montgomery had identified, she was certainly onto *something.*

The reason that I felt so secure in that judgment was, frankly, because of my own recent work in near-death studies. At the time Carol called me I had finished about two-thirds of my forthcoming book, *Heading Toward*

Omega: Near-Death Experiences and Human Evolution,
which deals chiefly with the transformations in the lives of
near-death survivors following their near-death experiences (NDEs) and with the larger, collective meaning of
those transformations for humanity as a whole. And in
many of Ruth Montgomery's cases which involved near-
death crises, she was finding precisely the same kind of
dramatic life changes in her subjects as I had with my own
near-death survivors. Indeed, several of the people she
identified as "Walk-ins" provided even stronger and more
compelling evidence of extraordinary transformations than
some of my own best examples! So while I found myself
dubious about her interpretation, I was decidedly envious
of her case history material. And, in any case, the parallels
between her findings and mine simply were too plain to be
denied.

So I capitulated and told Carol, "Yes."

It wasn't only because of my inability to dismiss the
relevance of Ruth Montgomery's findings from my mind
that I accepted Carol's invitation. It was also—and primarily, I think—that I could in no way dismiss *Carol.*

Although she and I have only met once—and then it was
briefly at a conference—we have been corresponding for
some years. I first heard from Carol in 1980 when she wrote
to describe her 1958 near-death experience—an event, as
this book now makes clear, that was the turning point in
her life. I was deeply moved by reading her powerful ac-
count of this experience and wrote to her to express my appreciation for her beautiful narrative. As we corresponded,
I grew familiar with Carol's work and life and followed,
albeit at a distance, her developing career with great interest and admiration. Even in those early days of our friendship, it was already clear to me that Carol was a woman
whose all too evident gifts—intellectual, psychic and spiritual—were bound to lead her to a position of national
prominence in New Age cirlces. And her recent accomplish-
ments as a writer, lecturer and minister have certainly
established her reputation at that level beyond any ques-

tion. Yet, it is in this book that Carol reveals for the first time the *basis* of her remarkable gifts which are responsible for her influential role in the New Age Movement. When I read her story—the story of her life *since* her near-death experience—I knew that, despite my wavering, it was, after all, right for me to write this forward. It was Carol herself who had finally dissolved all doubts.

Not only is this an important book for reasons I will shortly make clear, it is a deeply courageous one. Carol's story is of course unique but it fits a *pattern* I have observed in quite a number of near-death survivors I know. Most have been reluctant to speak too freely of some of the inner changes that they feel were triggered by their own NDEs. The fear of disbelief, ridicule or even scorn is still a sensitive issue for many near-death survivors and it is a factor that tends to make them reticent to speak out about the deeper implications of their experience. Carol Parrish-Harra, however, has now come along to speak for the many who have been silent. And the spiritual growth process she describes and the conclusions to which it has led her will, I'm sure, serve as familiar points of references for many others who have been thrust through a NDE or some other spiritual experience into an entirely new mode of being.

Carol has come to a deep understanding of the meaning of her own experience through a process of personal maturation which has led her to reflect upon its broader significance for all humanity as we move toward the end of this millenium. Through my own work with hundreds of near-death survivors, I have been forced to grapple with precisely the same issues that Carol has had to confront and have *independently reached a conclusion that is virtually identical to hers*. Carol's comes out of the matrix of her own life, mine derives from my research data, but on this matter we speak as though with a common voice.

I will not spoil your reading by divulging here any of Carol's own views nor the way in which they were disclosed to her. I will only say that her story is packed with spiritual events and personages that will keep you deeply absorbed as her personal odyssey unfolds. Neither will I comment upon the strictly metaphysical portions of her book except to say that those who hunger for metaphysical truths will find much to chew on here. And you will have to make up your own mind of course whether Carol is indeed a "Walk-in" or has perhaps simply come into her own authentic being to which her pre-NDE life had not granted expression.

Actually, Carol herself prefers the term "messenger" to that of "Walk-in"—and so do I. To me, it is in fact Carol's message that constitutes the ultimate, pre-eminent value of her book. I am personally convinced, moreover, that it is not only her message but *the common message* of the people with whom I have been working these past six years. As such, it is not just an important message; it is an absolutely *urgent* one which we can no longer afford to disregard. If we hear this message *and heed it,* the future of our life on this planet may be saved from the grim fate that so many fear. The fact that Carol speaks for many—8 million adult Americans are now estimated to have had a near-death experience—forces us to consider her words most carefully. Because she shows us how and why we may, indeed must, foster the development of a loving and caring human species on earth, she is truly a messenger of hope. It is up to all of us to contribute to the realization of the vision Carol has shown us to be within our power.

Kenneth Ring
January 27, 1983
Storrs, Connecticut

Introduction

The Awakening Of A Walk-In

In this book I attempt to describe the woman I once was and the reasons for the change to the woman I am now. In the interval I was engaged in a painful process which I could not understand or explain. I now know it was the time when the original Carol "died" and a new Carol arrived to begin her special task. The in between years of awakening to the new personality were lonely, confusing and frightening.

Today, 24 years later, I am ready to share this experience. I do this fully aware that some will scoff and that some will question. At times, when I write about those extraordinary years, it is very painful. However, I have completed this book because the time has come to do so. It is addressed to those who have the eyes with which to see and the ears with which to hear.

"To awaken" is a term commonly used in religious, esoteric and spiritual teachings. My own religious and esoteric education has made clear the concept expressed by that term: we "wake up" to the fact of God, to the knowledge that we are more than our bodies, emotions or mind. Ultimately, as expansion of consciousness occurs, we integrate these aspects into a wholeness, a harmonious, smoothly operating personality into which spiritual inspiration can also flow. With this story of mine I will suggest to you another dimension, another connotation to "waking up."

In referring to ancient teachings, a rare phenomenon was spoken of which challenges modern religious thought. In the Christian Bible it is referred to with these words:

"Be not forgetful to entertain strangers; for thereby some have entertained angels unawares." (Hebrews 13:2)

There are other writings lesser known, which speak of the Hierarchy (or Elder Brothers) of humanity who guide the earth both from the spiritual levels and from communication with adepts living on the earth. The adepts are those awakened beings who have mastered the process of integrating the personality to provide vehicles through which spirit may flow undistorted. These teachings speak of the externalization of the Hierarchy. This means that from time to time, when humanity's needs are great, some of the elder brothers (adepts), come into physical bodies in order to be of special service to mankind.

Recently, in *Strangers Among Us,* Ruth Montgomery presented these ideas to the public coining the word "Walk-ins" to identify souls coming in at this time to serve humanity in specific ways. These Walk-ins enter the body of certain unhappy persons wishing to die who give their consent and cooperation at a spiritual level. In this way, service to humanity is rendered by the departing one. The new soul who has chosen to enter into the living body vehicle is also required to render spiritual service.

Some readers will remember just such a story dramatically told by Lobsang Rampa in a series of books published since 1960. In his story certain recurring themes appear to stand out. His work supports the thought that the eastern and western spiritual paths have peculiarities unique to each respective tradition. Yet there consistently remains the reference in each to an agreement between certain beings in which one gives up his/her body to another. In this story of my body exchange I attempt to share the trauma involved and the reason for such beings coming in, plus a plea to humanity to listen.

Today this change of body inhabitants is believed to be happening more often. Spiritual wisdom teaches that there is nothing wasted in the Universe and that it functions with perfect economy of energy. The exchange of which I write may be seen as an application of these laws. If we believe all things work together for the good of all, we may begin to see the wisdom of certain incoming souls taking over the body created by another to serve a purpose useful to humanity. This process gains in importance at certain historical periods, especially when the incoming soul has a unique mission pertinent to a particular time, such as in the needful present day.

Personally I find the term "Walk-in" a bit sensational and not the term I would have chosen, but I trust in its directness. It has gotten the attention of many. I prefer the term "messenger" because I think it recognizes the reason for such an exchange in a more meaningful way. I challenge you to ponder the implications laid before you.

I have waited twenty-four years before speaking for a good reason. I have sought to build the necessary credibility, demonstrating my sincerity and honesty through the expression of my life. It is my personal integrity I place before you on these pages.

> With love,
> Carol W. Parrish-Harra

God, my Mother and my Father,
Sometimes You hide Your face from me
Behind the fog of Your clouds.
Sometimes I cannot see because of the darkness.
Then I must find within myself
The Light to show me The Way.
The clouds come and go,
The sun always shines.
I think it is my challenge to know the sun
    beyond the clouds,
Shining in Peace, even while it storms.
I seem to find You here, too, within my heart.
Dear God, You are truly everywhere.

November 12, 1981

Section I

Waking Up

Chapter 1

The Exchange Occurs

A secret, once it is told, is readily known. A mystery, once revealed, is more difficult to comprehend. A Truth, once unveiled, is a mystery until, through a gradual process of inner growth, its significance becomes perceivable.

Twenty-four years ago a great and awesome mystery engaged me in a life process which was to become both bewildering and beautiful; both astonishing and agonizing. Herman Melville has written that in everyone "resides certain wondrous, occult properties . . . why by some happy but rare accident . . . may chance to be called forth." This calling forth occurred for me during the birth of a child in 1958. I was to awaken from the anesthetic to a life more different than I could have ever dreamed.

Enlightened beings, who, after successfully completing numerous incarnations, have attained sufficient awareness of the meaning of life can forego the time-consuming process of birth and childhood, returning directly to adult bodies.

A Walk-in is a high-minded entity who is permitted to take over the body of another human being who wishes to depart. Since a Walk-in must never enter a body without the permission of its owner this is not to be confused with those well-publicized cases (such as were described in The Three Faces of Eve, The Exorcist, *et. al.) in which multiple egos or evil spirits are vying for possession of an inhabited body. The motivation for a Walk-in is humanitarian. He returns to physical being in order to help*

1

*others help themselves, planting seed-concepts that will
grow and flourish for the benefit of mankind.*[1]

In her book, Ruth Montgomery continues her explanation, stating that the personality originally created by the
person choosing to leave is left intact for the incoming soul.
Specifically, this means the body, the emotional make-up,
the intellect and the memory are available to the incoming
soul. He/she must now use this already developed form and
seek to impress its personality with new vitality and
ultimately exchange the old personality patterns with its
own. This alteration is done slowly and is partially responsible for the trauma experienced by the incoming one. During this transition time, imagine the puzzling "difference"
that is felt at times by those around this changing personality! I have found that during this critical period the
greatest challenge for the Walk-in (for clarity I will continue to use this word coined by Ruth Montgomery) is not
to forget his/her mission and the reason for taking on the
role. In addition to these formidable tasks, there is the further obligation to complete some of the responsibilities in-
curred by the outgoing soul.

Probably there is no better time for such a change to occur than during what today is called the Near Death Experience, generally a result of a serious illness or accident.
It was in this manner that Carol, the original builder and
creator of the physical, emotional and mental form, could
depart and donate the vehicle to an incoming soul.

At this point I would like to share with you the Near
Death Experience that occurred in 1958. It totally changed
the life of the Carol personality, producing a whole new
assurance about the continuity of life. I know there is
something more than earthly life; I have experienced a part
of the other and I remember it. I wish to share with you
this secret of mine; a mystery which gradually unfolded.

During the birth of a child, young Carol got into diffi-

---

[1]*Strangers Among Us*, Ruth Montgomery (New York: Fawcett Crest, 1979),
pp. 11-12.

culty as she was given sodium pentothal, a relatively harmless drug for most people. An allergic reaction occurred. The lungs collapsed and the spiritual body separated from the physical and moved to a place of observation near the ceiling. She looked down upon the physical body and did not know for a moment who it was; then she realized that it was "herself." Watching the hurried efforts of the doctors and nurses, young Carol saw the baby born, recognizing it was a little girl and realizing she was the woman giving birth. From a place near the ceiling, where she was drifting like a bobbing balloon, she saw a silvery umbilical cord attaching the "floating person" to the top of the head of the "physical person" on the operating table. It was incredible and impossible to understand!

Suddenly there was a brief moment of fast motion, a whirling, and she found herself "out" in what seemed to be vast space with no sight of her physical self on the operating table. It was cool and beautiful and lighted by lovely stars and she felt a dear, sweet peace.

Relief embraced and enveloped her. The knowledge that she had left behind a life of pain, sadness and impossible tasks helped sweep her rapidly into the open space of the heavens. For a critical, rapturous moment, two entities met and she passed on.

I, the incoming soul, remember standing before a Being with a magnificent presence. I could not see an exact form, rather a radiation of light that lit the heavens and it spoke with a voice that held the deepest tenderness one could ever imagine. The voice said, "Look." I looked into an area that suddenly was enclosed with a large golden frame. As I watched, a bright falling star moved from an upper corner and continued slowly, gently, across the framed space. As it got to the lower corner, its light went out. The voice said, "My child, do not be disturbed. Death makes no difference in the pattern. If you are, you always will be."

At this moment, as this loving and powerful Being spoke to me, I understood vast Truths, far beyond ordinary ability to explain. I understood life/death, and instantly, any fear I had as an incoming soul was ended. There was a totality, a completeness in the realization that I was being strengthened in order to retain and to share, in time, these life-enriching principles.

For what seemed to be endless time I experienced this Presence. The Light Being, pure, powerful, all-expansive, was without form. It can be said that great waves of awareness flowed to me and into my mind. As I responded to the revelations I was given, I knew them to be Truth. There was a complete trust and understanding of what these words meant as I stood in that moment of preparation.

Whole Truths revealed themselves to me. Waves of thought, ideas greater and purer than the young Carol had ever tried to comprehend, penetrated my being. Without effort I absorbed clear thoughts in total wholeness. And I, in that magnificent Presence, understood it all. I realized that consciousness is life. Human beings will live in and through much and this living consciousness, which we know is behind our personality, will continue. I knew now that the purpose of life does not depend on an individual; it has its own purpose. New serenity entered my being.

As this occurred, an intensity of feeling rushed through me, as if the light that surrounded that Being was bathing me, penetrating every part of me. As I absorbed the energy, I sensed what I can only describe as bliss. That is such a little word, but the feeling was dynamic, rolling, magnificent, expanding, ecstatic . . . BLISS. It whirled about me and entered my chest, flowing through me. I was immersed in love and awareness for an ineffable time.

In the bright light of this Presence, courage welled up in me and the wonder of life and the secrets in the universe filled me as revelations which I was to recall at a proper time in the future. I felt bouyant and strong, prepared to let life lift and guide me.

An intense rush of energy penetrated every part of my being. As I absorbed the pulsating love, bliss became my nature. I was whirled downward . . . outward. The feelings were dynamic, rolling, magnificent, expanding. Time rushed about in great swirls. There was no place to catch hold . . . suddenly, darkness. The heaviness of the physical body made itself felt. I let myself rest in that darkness, the tender, caring darkness of a womb. I was enfolded in the memory of great love.

A part of me was regaining physical consciousness; another part of me held back still floating somewhere, trying to hold on to the love, peacefulness and safety of the minutes just past.

The medical hands which turned my body pulled me outward from the inner world of peace. For a brief moment I remained poised, a being aware of two worlds, not quite committed to the outer. In my innermost being I questioned, "Do I really dare to do this?" The echoing answer was, "Yes!" It was done.

Eagerly I opened my eyes to look into the future. Eagerly I embraced new life in the physical body. As the new Carol, I would be able to share, to grow and to serve. As I opened my eyes I saw the relief on everyone's face. I told them, "It was wonderful, beautiful, don't be so concerned. I am fine!"

Words rushed out of my mouth: about the bright light; about how I understood the meaning of life; about the power and the clarity I had experienced. The doctor patted me and told me to forget it, adding, "Often people hallucinate under medication . . . it doesn't mean anything, rest now. You've had quite a time."

My eyes filled with tears as I looked at the faces around me, each set of eyes closed to the words and beauty I tried to share. No one there could or would believe. There was no one who wanted to hear what had happened, what wonderful things I had to tell.

I closed my eyes and quickly floated into sleep, trying to recall that feeling of real peace, the last I would feel for many years. Some part of me realized at that moment that I had a lot to do before I could share with others my precious experience. I knew there would be much to bear before I could make myself better understood. It was a relief to escape into sleep.

Chapter 2

Fighting To Remember

In the next few hours as I slept following the NDE, my husband was again called to the hospital because it was believed I was dying. It would be the next day before I could get hold of the physical world and begin to feel any attachment to it. Later, when I spoke of the experience, some of my words to my husband were prophetic, although I didn't know it at the time.

"Everything is different . . . I'm not like I used to be. I know so much more now; I see things differently. I don't feel the same. I know I can't go on as I used to be!"

In the days that followed my return home from the hospital with Susan, our newest child, the hours rushed by as I cared for our children; the new baby was our sixth. With only one child in school, there was too much work for me to have the luxury of time to ponder upon all of the experience. However, it was always present somewhere in my consciousness: the transcendant awareness that such beauty, love and understanding existed. Yet, then, it seemed to be out of my reach. It wasn't until years later that I would understand this transition period, the time when, as an incoming soul, I would struggle to reshape the former Carol's personality and complete some of her responsibilities.

My world demanded unceasing physical exertion and I could hardly stagger through each day. The only time I dared to stop was to nurse Susan and rock her a bit. Even then, Mary Beth, barely thirteen months, wanted to be rocked also. If I did that, what about three-year-old Michael? If it hadn't been for our five-year-old, Brenda, I never would have been able to meet the challenges waiting for me each day. Her love for the other children helped me very much. Her tender care of Susan, so tiny and new, allowed me the time to rock Mary Beth so that she wouldn't grow to resent this baby sister.

The exhaustion was not new. Even before becoming pregnant with Susan I remembered how young Carol was reaching the end of her rope. Three months before the NDE she had learned her husband was having an affair with one of her close friends. It became so serious the two of them had left their families to be together . . . although both reconsidered and returned home to their mates, the pain of this experience had been the last straw. Carol now wanted to die. Believing her seemingly endless efforts were useless and that she would never be able to manage, she had no hope. She and Bill were so completely unhappy.

Feeling trapped, she had given consideration to taking her life. She also had discussed practicing birth control, but her husband ridiculed the thought. Questioning her faith and selfishness, he challenged, "What kind of woman are you?" Wasn't it she who had convinced him to convert to Catholicism, who had wanted him to be baptized and who had him agree to have their children raised in that faith? Calling her "cheap and selfish" and accusing her of daring to "chicken out" of her own committment, his sharp words stung as he yelled, "You'd better do some talking to God!" Shaken by such anger, bewildered and exhausted, young Carol agreed to do as he said and made the effort, although often in bed at night she lay awake fervently wishing to be dead.

Now with the memory of that previous Carol still intact, I was remembering the struggle of the preceding months, even though my feeling nature seemed disconnected and unable to function. At that point in my experience I was unable to find the words with which to communicate to people that the most precious moments of my entire life had come when it appeared to everyone that I was dying; I couldn't understand it, so how could I explain it to others?

But . . . I had EXPERIENCED those moments and I did question whether they were given to me because I had wanted to die so very much. I also wondered if my mind had been so unkind as to tease me by showing me all that beauty; and then taking it away. Or perhaps, I thought, I had not proven worthy of the heaven I was shown: that sublime place of indescribable comfort, love and understanding.

In that heaven-place I was so strong. There I understood everything that mattered and I knew what I was to accomplish! It was made completely clear to me that everything has a purpose; those things which seem useless or accidental are, in fact, of real consequence. In that heaven-space I understood that life and death had a different connotation . . . a significance beyond the traditional perceptions. I learned it was unnecessary to feel much urgency about them. There, in the warmth of total love, I was also shown my children and told that they would grow up, with or without me; all would work out.

However, even with this exquisite memory, I was still having difficulty coping with the myriad daily claims to my energy. I struggled to get back into the rhythm of my family duties. A strange detachment held me close. I viewed my husband, my children, my parents, as if I scarcely knew them. My ever present question was: "Would I ever love them again as I had before?" My incessant internal questioning produced no immediate answer.

Following the NDE all emotions seemed less focused. I knew I loved the six children. Yet daily affairs (situations) seemed to be less critical. I felt no one could understand my feelings because they were so pliant. It seemed that I could love any child I saw as much as I loved my own. I loved other persons with the same feeling I had for my parents. I didn't feel less protective of my own family, it was that I was feeling involved with everyone else as well! I often struggled to shut off some of these feelings that would rush into and over me because they were so powerful they were frightening to me.

At other times, I would be strangely detached, observing a painful or emotionally charged situation from an impersonal curiosity. In these situations, often the question I would ask or the response I would make seemed out of place. I realized I seemed aloof to others at some moments and yet found at other times I was so immersed in new feelings of love that I had to struggle to separate myself. Observing these emotional shifts, in time I was able to see the personal, possessive feelings give way to an impersonal, general acceptance. The shift toward more peace increased when I began to believe in and accept my own individuality. I gradually stopped judging myself so harshly. As I gave more acceptance to my own feelings, a new-found trust emerged. I found I could be comforted by the pool of inner knowledge upon which I pondered. This growing sense of security was a buffer from the painful memories of the former Carol with which I still lived.

In this transition period, as I continued the painful task of working with the energy of the previous Carol personality, Bill and I quarrelled more often and I became withdrawn, angry and silent. I would pout because I couldn't put my pain and detachment into words. I was unable to explain how hurt and tired and lonely I was. Frequently I retreated into silence, doing only what I had to do to get through each day. Occasionally, the memory from the first Carol's personality would cause me to wish to die and finish with life. Even though we attempted to make our marriage work, it was obvious Bill wanted to be free. However, I made it clear that I had "talked to God" as he had commanded, and I would never be able to give him a divorce. He loved the children, but he wanted a wife who was free and willing to go out with him, drinking and laughing and enjoying his interests. I was not the right person for him and it was obvious to both of us that our marriage was a mistake. We did not talk about our incompatibility. Somehow the situation seemed out of our hands.

Young Carol's view of life was so different from Bill's. She was a young woman who had always struggled for parental acceptance. She sought her parent's praise which came when her house was neat and her children were clean and good; when she was outshining the other young mothers her parents knew. She worked very hard to hear her mother say, "Carol outdoes me. I don't know how she does it all. Her house is so clean, and with all those kids. . . ." During this transition, that kind of compliment was still a part of what kept me going, struggling even harder on those days when I didn't escape into silence. It should not be difficult to imagine that with all these pressures, plus the inner inexplicable experiences I was having, most of my energy was expended in meeting the daily challenge of maintaining my sanity.

However, the moments when I would touch into new inner events were increasing. These caused me to remember young Carol's childhood and her grandparents. Daddy Parrot, Carol's grandfather, told her, "You can do anything, be anything. Just do it." He was also one person who knew she wasn't lying when she "saw" things that other people didn't. Remembering his consistently wise advice helped sustain and guide me as I underwent the strange and confusing awakening process. He had said, "It's okay to 'see' what you do, just don't tell everything you know, Carol. It will be easier." He was right! Remembering the unconditional love of these grandparents was now helping me feel better about myself. They had given the great gift of letting young Carol tell them about those things she "felt and saw" which were unknown to other people. It was to be through my inner life experiences in this trying transitional time that I would grow to understand what they had known: young Carol had been a psychically sensitive child.

Powerful psychic experiences began to occur after the NDE. In the beginning they made me ever more lonely, even as they propelled me toward my improbable future. Gradually, however, the personality began to accept the incoming Walk-in influence, and I found my attitudes and emotions becoming easier to express.

Sometimes, sitting in our yard watching the children, I would feel a love so powerful my chest flooded with emotion. I would recall the Living Love that flowed to me from the Light Being and I was curious, for it now seemed to be causing me to feel so deeply about the people around me. It was a caring very different from the sentimental love young Carol had felt. As an example, one day Aunt Lee, our neighbor, came across the street to talk to me about her sister who was critically ill. As she began to cry, all the energy in my body seemed to go toward her. I reached out and held her, wanting to stop her pain more than anything in the world. I wasn't even embarrassed at my tenderness, although this kind of reaction had been totally unusual for me. Young Carol had not been in the habit of responding so openly to another's problems. Somehow I realized this new experience was related to the Light Being. Prior to that meeting Carol had always felt too busy and had let the rest of the world take care of itself. She had been certain the world wasn't hers to fix: "I have enough to do, thank you." But, after the experience in the delivery room, I found the new Carol beginning to cherish others, feeling I should do something about everything!

Of course, that made no sense at all. I couldn't get my own work done or solve my own problems, so how could I be the one to settle everyone else's? It began to be more and more of a relief to sit silently, alone, being quiet with my own thoughts soothing me. I was feeling so very much out of place. It seemed to make people uncomfortable to hear about my unusual feelings and thoughts. I met no other person with whom I could talk about the light in my head, the intensity of the feelings that were evoked by beauty, or my knowledge of the presence of God.

Another example of a profound psychic occurrence took place a few months after Susan's birth, when I was at Mass. As communion time approached, the bells rang. This was my favorite moment: the priest held the Host high in the air. I struck my breast: "Dear God, how I love Thee, how I love Jesus, how I adore Thee!" Suddenly it seemed the ceiling opened up!

A rich dazzling feeling of love exploded within me. My

eye fastened on the Host as it shattered into light, the colors leaping and dancing, the rays flashing from wall to wall. The church was encompassed, filled with breathtaking brilliance. It proclaimed the power of the Mass and the Host, beyond doubt!

I couldn't move; my body and eyes were rigidly fixed. People had to climb over me. I was unable to slide back into my seat. I remained kneeling, transfixed . . . the ecstasy flowing through my body and my mind. I had no understanding as to where the brilliance was coming from, nor did I know what was happening to me. I could only participate with this power, kneeling there until the service was over.

Afterward, Father came to me to see if I was all right. He told me to get up and go home. I tried to talk, but only tears came. That convinced him I should leave immediately and without talking! It was obvious he didn't know what had happened to me either. Subsequently, when I tried to talk with him about the occurrence, his response to my questions intimidated me. He really didn't understand. Was I too crazy or too ignorant to be heard? It was unbelievably difficult for me; I suspected that my husband and Father were right; I had to get a grip on myself or I'd end up in the hospital.

Time does heal, thank goodness, and I hung on to life and kept future questions to myself. An incoming soul with a new personality, I struggled with the many daily responsibilities as I also endeavored to hold in my memory the impression of myself rushing forward into this full life expression, promising most readily over my shoulder that, "Yes, yes, I can do this!" In those moments I was rejoicing in the joy of entering into physical life and eager to strive to meet the challenges of the times. I knew that a time of great opportunity was fast approaching on earth. I was prepared for all that would come. I knew why and even how. My greatest challenge was to remember all this and I would tell myself daily, "It will work out!"

I would carefully reflect upon what I knew deep within

and I would review the vast understanding I wanted to offer. Just as the seed of a flower contains all the knowledge of how to bloom and how to create, I contained the knowledge of the many levels of existence. I understood that I carried all the strengths, insights and knowledge I would need. It has been indelibly etched into my memory at the exchange. Stepping into that Light with its bountiful energy swirling through my consciousness had been the most important moment of all.

In the presence of the Light Being I realized the physical body I was to enter would have to be rebuilt and strengthened, but the young Carol's memory and the sensitive intuitive nature of her basic self would serve me well. Her previously intimidated personality would give way to my new influence. The old devotional temperament would gradually become better balanced. The heavy dedication to duty, "even if it kills me," would always be a factor, but greater understanding would make possible a new objectivity. In esoteric terms this may be said another way: the strong ray six[2] emotional influence would give way to a tempered ray two.[3] The ability to see both sides of an issue would be cultivated. The previous heavy programming of absolutes of right and wrong, as well as the feelings of inadequacy would be reworked as I impressed the vehicle with new energy.

As the next two to three years passed, gradually I noticed the change. Eventually I became aware that I was becoming a more caring person . . . that life was becoming more desirable to me. SOMETHING was happening . . . I was feeling good and gaining in energy. I was also confused by what this meant. Occasionally, at the very perimeter of my mind I would KNOW how my life was important. I could sense the pieces of understanding and guidance bringing all of these experiences into focus. I fought to remember that "something" which I had to do that was planned just for me. I had a special reason to be alive and I would surely find that reason someday!

---

[2]*Initiation of the World*, Vera Stanley Alder (New York: Samuel Weiser, 1973).
[3]Ibid.

Chapter 3

When The Student Is Ready

My outer life passed day by day, busy and productive. However, a certain part of my attention always seemed to be focused inward. I began to feel life unfolding with more harmony. I could feel I was getting onto a track. The many synchronicities became more frequent. The help I needed came from many sources. Later, one of these would be a teacher, Ann Manser, who triggered the "knowing" even more strongly. The right books began to appear. Meditation patterns became established and the insights that occurred satisfied the restlessness so I could feel steady and calm.

As I had explained after the NDE the relationship with my husband remained awkward, yet polite. He experienced acute guilt over the danger of my physical safety. He loved the children and couldn't understand his wife. He wanted to be free, yet neither of us saw a way out. We avoided speaking of our incompatibility.

The pain of the previous months was etched into the relationship. While every attempt to forgive and forget was made, no new bond grew. The heavy feelings of responsibility and acute awareness of committment continued and lingered for years. The new baby was taken to be baptized by a young mother standing alone, with god parents almost unknown to her, while an unhappy father, confused by the struggle of life, stayed home.

For the next few years, from time to time, my husband made an effort to relate to a wife who seemed growing off into some world of ideas and feelings too hard to understand. The wife, once content to stay home, became a career woman. The mother so often pregnant now spoke of education and success. The shift in view became increasingly complex to a family where intense ambition and powerful goals were not encouraged. My confidence grew as new talents emerged. The search for outer capabilities encouraged the new inner nature to believe in itself.

In the years between 1958 and 1968 the struggle to discover myself found me kneeling in the confessional crying, pleading for directions, angry in my belief that the priest had answers and wouldn't help me. Devouring *Imitation of Christ* until I could quote it to myself, I tried to stop the perceptive insights that came for they seemed to be illogical. I had no one to turn to for understanding. I was certain however, that it was increasingly important that I become acceptable, capable and strong.

One day as joy flooded my being and I quieted myself, I entered the prayerful attitude of quiet receptivity and a picture clearly showed itself in my mind. A small ball of shadows expanded, opening like a fan of peacock feathers. Alert, I watched with my sense of imagination. In a few minutes it faded away. I felt a vague sense of remembrance, as if I had recognized something helpful. I would return a number of times to the pleasant inner quiet before the sign would come again. As months passed this particular symbol would strike a chord of wonder for me. It seemed a priceless gift. I did not know what it was, but I returned to hunt for its peace and fascination almost daily.

Between November 1958 and 1965 I gave birth to four more children. The first, a son, was delivered prematurely Nov. 6, 1959, a tiny human form who just wasn't ready to live. I experienced an incredible feeling of surprise, then failure, for I had thought everything was fine. My spirits had been up and inwardly I had returned to a less confused and unquestioning state of mind. To my relief I had been developing more positive feelings about life in general. My grief was not acute; it was really vague, creeping upon me at unlikely moments. I had a problem looking at it squarely. The worst moments were when I accepted the loss of a son as my personal failure. I felt miserably inadequate. My desire for a boy had been intense as we already had five daughters and only one son. Also, I believed I had failed our older son by not giving him a much needed and desired brother.

In October 1960 I delivered another beautiful baby girl to our family. I experienced no concern for the sex of this baby, only the burning desire to have a child to make up for that other failure. Two years later, in November, 1962, the little son and brother arrived. It was a remarkably speedy delivery with very little pain, but it was followed by severe hemorrhaging. Amazingly, this would prove to be the next important step in my waking-up process.

As the doctor was talking to me and advising me to have surgery, I REMEMBERED I was supposed to have one more child, a girl. I had promised to do so. I would not allow the surgery, for in some part of my consciousness I recalled my agreement with the Light Being. It was vague, but I KNEW—I was confident; it didn't matter that the doctor and others thought me stubborn and foolish. I would give birth to another girl!

This shocking recall set up another round of wondering. The only framework I had for such an obligation was the idea that I HAD PROMISED GOD. I could not break my vow.

It was April 6, 1965, when the baby girl arrived as "pre-arranged." She was lovely, lively and a feeling of success flooded me. I now had fulfilled that part of my committment. My heart sang with joy!

As my sense of security developed, I listened more and more to the sound of the wee small voice within. It spoke to me through a developing stream of dialogue which gave me insights to both myself and the world around me.

In 1962 I had become increasingly concerned about a particular look Mary Beth would have for a few seconds from time to time. I had tried for three or four months to determine her problem. She was now five, usually animated and active, yet at times, for a split second, with no other noticeable change of expression, the light would go out of her eyes. I had tried to point this out to her father and her grandmother.

I took her to our family pediatrician and had her examined. He could find nothing. One afternoon she was playing tether ball with me. Glancing up at just the right moment I saw the dull instant of no-light pass over her face. Her timing for the ball was thrown off and it smacked into her face. I cried aloud, "What is that?" and heard an instant response, "Epilepsy." I glanced around to see who had answered me, but no one else was with us. As I washed Mary Beth's face and dried her tears, my heart beat rapidly. What if it were epilepsy? As soon as I could put her back to play with the other children I called the doctor. I asked him point-blank, "Can Mary Beth have epilepsy? Is that what I see?" He began to calm me, responding, "Don't worry, Carol, our examination didn't indicate Mary Beth has epilepsy." Again I pressed him, "How would you test her if you thought she did?" He explained that she'd go to a Saint Petersburg hospital and have an EEG, adding, "You don't need to do that. Your imagination is running away with you because of your concern." Yet, for her sake, and mine, I needed to know. I had to know if I could trust the inner voice which had answered my impulsive cry.

"Please give her the tests!" I pleaded. Finally, to pamper me, he agreed. I hung up the phone. I had taken a giant step; I had followed the advice of my inner guidance.

Mary Beth had the EEG; petit mal was diagnosed. The doctor was astonished and questioned how I could have known. I never told him more than, "I just knew." But from then on, he and I had a closer bond. Mary Beth was put on medication and in a short time the condition was under control. For the next five years she continued on medication and had no problems.

Now I understood something of great import: I knew that "that voice" could, and would, give me information I could get nowhere else.

The deeply devotional nature continued in the joy of weekly Mass. A special strength was gleaned in these years by being a member of the Night Adoration Society of the Sacred Heart of Jesus. Slipping out of bed to light a candle to pray and to chant awakened the fervor to know that mystery that was hidden from daily view. I was becoming increasingly aware of the flow of energy that would build in my chest at certain times and the power of understanding matters not limited to daily life began to be revealed. "Just knowing" emerged.

Sometimes in the midst of night adoration, the feeling of a pounding force would rush upward through the body. As my body swayed, the shoulders would stiffen and slightly arch as my mind swirled into that loving bliss. Sometimes later I would awaken lying on the floor, cheeks well wet with tears. Sometimes I would realize I'd open my mouth and sweet music would come. Sometimes I would hear a voice tell me things about life, its purpose, and myself.

The confessional rang with my tears and my despair. It was no use. No one cared. Father gave me absolution and felt he had done his best. He probably had.

The door, so locked to help from outside, opened to an increased sense of achievement. The physical life improved. I was capable. Employment increased my self-esteem and provided the catalyst for a separation and divorce. Common sense made up for educated skills and the sense of meeting challenges was realized.

The years passed, and the once harried mother, lonely and worn, gave way to a busier woman, capable and getting stronger daily. I continuously studied night courses, learned to budget time and money, discovered talent and drive. With my attitude becoming more positive and my confidence increasing, I was receiving praise at my employment. I was truly learning I was capable and bright. Not a bad thing to find out at age 33 after ten children and a painful divorce! All of my illusions of being the perfect mother and homemaker were dissolving. The years of struggle were done. Bill and I had decided to let go. Both of us fought fear and guilt and struggled with the sense of defeat we carried.

But with my new sense of freedom I was able to be more true to myself. I had time to spend quietly, philosophically, to grow more secure with my own changes. The conflict within me came and went.

Developing a sense of philosophy, I read *Lives of Saints* and even began to discover Protestant mystics when, unexpectedly, help arrived.

No events were more significant to my own awakening to the inner nature and my own levels of self than my meetings with Rev. Leroy Zemke and Mrs. Ann Manser, now deceased, in St. Petersburg, Florida. I met Rev. Zemke at a chance meeting in a home in Clearwater, Florida, when invited to a discussion group. I slipped into the lovely suburban home just as the handsome young man began to write his topic on the blackboard. He carefully wrote "Astral Travel." I thought, "Oh God, another travelogue."

Within a few minutes I was on the edge of my seat listening to an explanation of a peculiar happening I experienced from time to time. At the break I pushed through the group to personally question Rev. Zemke. Emotion flooded me as I said to him, "Sir, I think you've saved my mind."

I learned Rev. Zemke was pastor of a metaphysical church, which I soon visited. It was a converted Little Theater with larger than life paintings on the walls and a flowered carpet on the stage. In this strange and unusual atmosphere I chose a seat in the very back. The evening program began with singing and a short lecture. The highlight, a demonstration of psychic impressions, caught me by surprise. I had never seen such a thing and when Rev. Zemke stepped down into the audience speaking into a lariat microphone, I was amazed. He immediately asked me to speak my name. After my response he began to describe most accurately my office, a personal situation and thoroughly overwhelmed me by saying, "Someday, young lady, you will stand in this very spot and do this exact thing. You're a natural psychic and don't know how to use your talent." As he moved on to attune to another person, with my heart pounding, I rushed out of there. I had wanted answers that would help me with my moods, loneliness, memories and confusions and I suddenly realized I was standing at the brink of that discovery.

It was on my next visit to the church, this time a Saturday afternoon social, that Ann Manser approached me with a mysterious remark, "Where have you been? I've been waiting for you."

Ann became my guide as I sorted through esoteric literature. A former Catholic herself, she helped me deal with the pain and loss I felt as I began to leave orthodox religion and entered into a life new with mystical awareness. She encouraged my life of prayer, meditation and a regular time for contemplation. Her understanding of "inner space, energies and symbology" answered my questions and my needs.

I safely shared my memories, my dreams, my visions. She tested my intuitiveness, my psychic impressions, my inner plane experiences. She led me in exercises, read my diary, encouraged me to believe in ideas as broad as found in science fiction.

Her wisdom could handle my most scary impressions and visions. Recall of other lives were no longer shocking. Ann demanded respect and logic. She demonstrated the refinement of a fine lady, the sincerity of a true spiritual teacher and the skill of a fine writer.

Ann took students on a one-to-one basis and shared with each as she felt so led. She guided the personal development of each of her "chicks" fervently. She accepted ideas of life in other dimensions and of other evolutions incarnating within the human family. She encouraged me to remember my NDE with great reverence. She supported my search for a greater understanding of the changes within myself, and when I asked, "Could I have died as one person and come back as another?" She said, "Why not? Who knows what God can do?"

Ann was hard to understand. She was critical of sloppy

work, eager to question and challenge and yet she allowed me to believe I was of another grouping here with a duty to perform. She also made it clear that an air of superiority reeked of ego and blocked the flow of intuitive knowledge. I believe Ann saw it as her personal duty to knock the air out of the sails of her students whenever she got the opportunity, which was rather frequently!

In 1969 one rarely heard such terms as auroscope,* or reading of the spiritual aura, which is what Ann called her interpretation of the Soul colors in the auric pattern of one to whom she attuned.

I was introduced to Sirius[4] at this time as a real force and relationship. The concept of spiritual family (evolution) group service became personal. I saw myself as one "on the spiritual path" with a reason for being. Ann encouraged a life of preparation with the guiding thought of, "When the student is ready the teacher shall appear." My understanding was that she appeared as an answer to my agony and prayers.

---

*See Chapter 7.

[4]*The Sirius Mystery,* Robert K. G. Temple (New York: St. Martin's Press, 1976).

Chapter 4

How This Can Be

Walk-ins are incarnating souls who take a short-cut into physical life. Instead of the usual route, fetus to adult, a Walk-in figuratively "walks in" to an already grown human body. The original occupant gives its body as a gift to an incoming soul so that it can save the time and energy usually required in the human maturing process.

The outgoing soul will be going about its business of living and learning in the spirit world just as all do when they leave behind the physical dimension. The best example I can offer is for us to realize a somewhat similar situation arises when a person is in a coma for a length of time.

Let's give this similarity some thought. If a person is unconscious for a long period, months or more, what is that soul doing? I have come to believe that the soul busies itself in the inner world just as the living do each night when they are behind the veil of sleep.

We have a consciousness thread (antahkarana), a life thread (sutratma), and a creative thread[5] and we must realize the purpose of each. The life thread brings the energy of spirit and matter together and charges the physical body with life force. The consciousness thread is the connection with the soul and it is this charge that is the lower part or you may say in another way, this is the spiritual link between the personality, the mental unit and the spiritual triad. The third thread is built by (the per-

---

[5]*Science of Becoming Oneself,* Torkom Sarydarian (California: The Aquarian Educational Group, 1969).

sonality) and is an extension of the life thread. This third creation aligns the centers and energies and is expanded as the person thinks in a higher or more noble way. This profound "linking up" is the work spiritual aspirants do by their contemplation and creative thinking and speaking. We must be aware it is the constantly expanding creation of the higher energies as they step down which causes soul infusion to take place within the personality.

Let's relate this to the physical body in a comatose state. What is going on? The body is alive, and yet there is no physical consciousness. The soul is still owner of the body and is keeping it charged through the life thread. The consciousness will be active on the astral or higher worlds. As long as the consciousness thread remains intact the patient may wake up later and return to full functioning. Many times this person can tell about being at another place or can accurately describe happenings in the room even though in a coma. Some tell about meeting someone they think they have known, such as a dead relative.

In the situation of a second soul being gifted with the physical mechanism, the consciousness thread is changed. The original creator releases the consciousness thread; with help the incoming soul is attached to the physical vehicle and the new force begins to flow into the mechanism. As a result of the new soul energy, the creative thread will begin to change and adjust to the new forces. If opportunities are favorable, rapid changes can occur. The remaining life thread raises questions for me. Is there still a tie to the departing soul? I am led to believe that the new soul also takes over that charge at the exchange. My own understanding of the "aka" thread, or psychic connection, as explained by Max Freedom Long,[6] causes me to believe this provides the mechanism for the blessings or good karma which flow to the vacating soul. The vehicle given to the incoming soul will vibrate with the energy of the out-

---

[6]*The Secret Science Behind Miracles,* Max Freedom Long (Missouri: Huna Research Publications, 1948).

going soul for a time while the incoming soul will be converting the body mechanism and personality frequencies to its own vibrations. It is in this period that I believe the new inhabitant finds confusion and conflict.

Let's think about this in another way. I have worn a pair of leather gloves for a long time and they have adjusted to the size and shape of my hands; then I give the gloves to another. Let us imagine that the new hands are a bit larger or differently shaped. In the beginning the gloves may not fit well, although they are nice. They must be worn awhile before they become comfortable; they probably will need to stretch. They will need to adjust before the new owner is at ease with them. Thus it goes with the personality gifted to another.

How interested is the outgoing soul in how the old personality fares under the direction of the new inhabitants? I think that differs. Just as we differ here, I believe souls differ on the spirit side. I think this is determined by level of development, reasons for leaving, etc. I believe most outgoing souls do little looking back. They are delighted to go on and while some may have real interest, my experience working with others I believe are Walk-ins proves the interest to look back is very minimal. I somehow think the wisdom of higher ones will be used to keep this to a minimum. Otherwise I could see grounds for grief and interference. The departing soul will be rewarded for rendering such service to those guiding humanity. The new positive soul energy will be released into the personality (the life thread, consciousness thread and creative thread), thus the energy will flow through the "aka" even to the departed one. This is a form of bonus for services rendered.

The outgoing soul will now be able to attend to opportunities for enrichment, learning, healing and comfort in the spirit world as any other freed soul. According to the evolution of the soul, the training will differ. If there has been much pain and negativity, and there is with the majority of those who "walk out," special care and handling in the area of healing is given. I think of how much need there is for support and encouragement here on earth as many have such hard experiences. I do believe these who have had such a discouraging time, yet have served a useful purpose are dealt with very tenderly.

Believing planet earth and humanity at present are facing a time of great testing, certain souls desire to have impact today upon those they can reach with their special message. By accepting a ready-made, grown body, even if imperfect or unhealthy, Walk-ins can make themselves heard much sooner. In exchange for this opportunity, these incoming souls agree to complete some unfinished tasks for the departing soul.

Walks-ins often complete the responsibilities to an aging parent, the raising of children and/or care of a mate when they come into the physical plane. Since most persons have ties that would be abruptly severed by death, this one coming in seeks to honor those responsibilities and if possible, repair or transform the life it has inherited.

The changing of souls creates a change in personality even as a throwing on of a light in a darkened room creates a different view. The incoming soul is challenged by the newness of the situation, plus in the greatest majority of cases, it will be months or years before he or she will realize what actually happened.

In the past this blankness has served well the incoming soul for it has had enough with which to cope. Some few persons in close proximity could detect the striking change, but this is generally neither the public nor family. If spiritually evolved help is available, esoteric philosophy softens the trauma with welcome help.

Human relationships are the most testy and the most dear, so the greatest responsibilities are to those interlocking ties to the personality. If these ties can be elevated to spiritual ties, to a loving in a higher or holier sense, they can adjust and remain rich as the life continues. If they were personality level only, or ties built on self-centeredness, power, ownership or manipulation, as the new person takes over the life the persons grow apart. On the non-physical plane the rule is that like attracts like, and when a life is designed to function from a particular level of reality it will loosen ties to other levels. This accounts for the many marriages that dissolve after a Walk-in enters the picture. If one's life energy is delegated intensely into a given direction, unless the mate can open to that same enthusiasm the relationship tends to come apart. Birds of a feather do flock together!

With the many challenges facing the Walk-in, he rejoices if the departing personality has built psychic sensitivity into its basic make-up. The advantage is that the life exchange is made less difficult as the basic personality can be impressed with the spiritual sense of the incoming soul.

Remembering the earlier comments about the creative thread, we realize the better the hook-up between levels of consciousness (and/or the vehicles), the clearer the soul can express. Thus we understand immediately the usefulness of a sensitive personality. While all Walk-ins have not necessarily managed to get sensitive or psychic vehicles, it stands to reason that a more delicately tuned mechanism is desirable. But it's important to remember the newly arrived soul may be able to have impact on the chakra energy centers and cause rapid changes. In many cases breakthrough after breakthrough occurs as the intense new soul learns to use the opportunities at hand. The word psychic can be misunderstood here unless we remember that psyche means "of the soul." Now we must expand the definition of a limited sensitivity to phenomena to mean soul pictures, impressions, thoughts and intuition. By using this expanded meaning we realize the joy of a soul blessed with an easy to impress basic mechanism.

It should also be apparent that "walking into" a healthy physical body would be especially desirable. However, most Walk-ins do have to strengthen or rebuild the vehicle they receive, as in many cases it is a near-death weakness which allows the transfer. Walk-ins have the further responsibility of impressing the new vehicle with higher spiritual energies. The first few years, seven to nine, are

critical for the Walk-in. Lives have to be rearranged to get
into the necessary posture to expedite their reason for entry. Finding encouragement and support among those they
encounter becomes a challenge. Since virtually no one dare
tell his story without it being used against him, these years
are often devastatingly lonely. This pain, however, causes
the newly arrived soul to search for the understanding
needed to reestablish contact with the higher world.

As a metaphysical teacher, I have been involved with
the study of the transformation process for several years.
Today, I find myself thinking of the Walk-ins as the
awaited "externalization of the hierarchy" which New Age
literature heralds. Many people around the world are
familiar with the books of H. P. Blavatsky, the Theosophical Society materials, the writings of Alice Bailey and
others, all of which consider the probability of help from entities from higher dimensions. This hierarchical externalization is a commonly accepted part of the present
change from the Piscean to the Aquarian Age. Others state
that the followers of the Christ will come to earth and take
their positions, ready to serve as needed. I choose to think
this is what we are seeing in our world today.

As I would explain the matter of the externalization of
the hierarchy, I would say it is manifesting presently in
two ways. The first, the Walk-ins have come to earth bringing with them their previous spiritual development so as to
be of service during humanity's imminent great crisis. Sec-
ondly, the hierarchy is also externalizing through the
emerging acceptance by many embodied individuals of
their own high consciousness. Persons busy with their
everyday lives are rapidly sensing their spiritual nature
and through the bombardment of many New Age ideas are
beginning to think deeply about ethical and spiritual concerns.

This type of self-examination awakens memories which
have been hidden from the conscious mind. As minds are
searched, examined and stretched, many persons find
reasons for accepting some part of the Truths previously

hidden from them. In recent years the idea of reincarnation has become more natural to us in the western world. The increasing knowledge in the natural sciences, and certainly the new dimensions in physics help many understand concepts which have been offered by the mystics through the ages.

The idea of souls coming in to help humanity should be rewarding, hopeful and encouraging, even if at first contact it seems hard to imagine. The movies such as "E.T." and "Close Encounters of the Third Kind" may plant seed thoughts which will help the Walk-in find a greater welcome and acceptance. While most Walk-ins are lacking the charm of an E.T., all are trying to present patterns for a new way of life of greater inspiration and love. They have challenging stories to tell and can teach humanity about expanding consciousness.

The last ten years have been ones of protection for the Walk-ins to help their missions become established. Everyday, the pieces suddenly come together for some Walk-ins, and they discover who they really are. This is both the end of one struggle and the beginning of another! These servants of humanity are required to be different, to say something, to give to others, each in their own way from their own resources. The spiritual nature previously hidden from both the public and the conscious mind must plant its seed, paint its picture, or speak its word.

Who will receive the treasures laid bare?

Section II
Preparation

Chapter 5

The Doors Fly Open

Earlier I mentioned that when I came home from the hospital I found myself feeling "detached." To a degree this detachment gradually subsided. Next I noticed a new intensity within. If I cared, I really cared! I observed that I virtually was never lukewarm emotionally.

This feeling of emotional identity would become strong whenever I'd see someone in pain. At times I would become very uncomfortable when this feeling would well up within me and I'd feel my heart go out to the one who was suffering. The sensation would be so strong I would feel swollen, most often in the chest area. Sometimes my back would arch slightly. It would become necessary to set up very straight to be comfortable.

Frequently I would ache to touch the person and if I could do so, I would then relax and feel more at one with the individual. As these impulses continued, I overcame my prior hesitancy and I have developed into a person who finds it both natural and comfortable to reach out, to touch and to hug.

Needless to say, these occurrences led me more and more into a healing ministry. I must add that this was an area I had thought I would avoid. Yet, the power of this impulse grew and flowed and in time manifested in a healing experience for my teenage daughter. The time, it seemed, had come.

A group I had been studying with asked me to get a certain minister to teach a Healing course for us. I agreed to do so and went to see this minister. He agreed to teach the

class. I joined the class as a matter of courtesy because I
had been the one to ask him, but I really was not comfortable with the subject. There was something about all this
feeling that stirred within myself that bothered me.

By the third week the Healing course had become very
important to me. I had a seventeen-year-old daughter in
the hospital, critically ill. That week, when we met, I was in
a hurry to get through with our class and go to the hospital
to visit my daughter. As the Lord would have it, the air-
conditioning man came that day to install the new system
in the church and I had to have the group at my house,
which delayed my going to the hospital. When the meeting
was over, the minister asked if we would please all join together in a prayer for my daughter. We prayed and for the
first time I thought I felt the energy of the group focus
itself. I did not feel anything more than this, but I was
aware of the sincerity of the group as they worked with her.
I left immediately and went to the hospital.

My daughter had hepatitis and was very seriously ill. She
had been on the critical list for two days. At the time I arrived at the hospital they were giving her injections to stop
the nausea. I went in and, as she lay there, I stood beside
her. She looked up at me and said, "Mother, heal me." I
looked at her and said, "Honey, only God can heal you!" She
looked straight at me and said, "Then why are you taking
that Healing course?" Right there and then it became a
very real thing for me. I said, "Honey, you close your eyes
and pray and I'll work with you." I went to the head of the
bed and began to place my hands over her and, as I did so,
I was trying to remember all of the diagrams I had seen
and the positions of what you do first, second, third and
fourth. I can only say one thing, I was sincere. Other than
that, I didn't know a technique, I worked over her entire
body, down to her feet. When I was through, I turned
around and looked at her . . . she had gone to sleep. I sat
down in a chair and I sincerely prayed that she would be
better. The time passed and I had to go home to take care
of my other children. From home I called the hospital at

eight o'clock and they said, "She has slept ever since you were here." Leaving her in their care, I went to bed.

The next morning—our house arises early and gets very hectic—I was getting the children ready for school and the phone rang. I went to the telephone and said, "Hello." The voice on the other end said, "Mother, I'm well." I asked, "Who is this?" I was so surprised! I jumped into my clothes and went quickly to the hospital. When I got there, I rushed in and the doctor was standing by her bed. He said, "Isn't it wonderful the way teenagers bounce back?"

At that point, I didn't know what I thought about healing. I was amazed at what had happened and yet, at the same time, when I talked to the minister who had been teaching our course, he said, "Well, that's what is supposed to happen!" In earnest, I began then to study healing.

Shortly after this, Rev. Leroy Zemke asked me to teach a Healing class. I was ready to try to understand the experiences that were happening around me. Suffice it to say, since that time, healing has seemed to me a natural way to show our love and caring.

The important point I would like to make in regard to healing work is how much it reminds me of the peace and love I felt within The Presence of the Light Being during the NDE. I often experience a loss of time while working with healing and awareness, and I seem to be focussed in this free flowing supply of bountiful love.

I like the definition of LOVE as Lots Of Vital Energy, because I believe many words are healing sources. I suggest peace, calmness, caring, energy transference and at-one-with. You can add your favorite. I think the healing flow brings what we need and is the agape love the world needs. I often hesitate to use the word love at all because of all the stickiness it can connote. My personal inner opening occurs for healing as I think the words and feel, "I care."

A great challenge I have struggled with consistently through the years since the NDE is my own impersonality. Young Carol was a private, sensitive person placing great emphasis upon her children, home and personal interests. She had made the remark, "If it doesn't happen in my yard it doesn't concern me." Very personally involved with the raising of her own children, whom she loved dearly, she had little to do with others. Her time and energy were under heavy demands at home with no time or energy left over for other interests. A home-body, she rarely left the house except on household errands and showed no interest in the world at large. Her nose was to the grind stone; her heart also was there.

Very shortly after the NDE the change of the emotional pattern of the new Carol began to be noticed. The more quiet and self-centered personality began to care for the world around her in a new way. The early detachment faded and a new intensity began, but this fervor was a nonconditional kind of love that loved both the children of the immediate household and the children of the neighborhood. It mattered that the children around the world were starving. It mattered if other person's parents were suffering as well. Suddenly the windows of the world were open and involvement was beginning everywhere. These changes were confusing and the ripples disturbed the status quo of the home and family life. It is important to understand the intensity of caring and yet the caring was not centered at a personal level.

Later you will see where Ann makes a reference to this particular quality in the aurascope she wrote about me, the incoming soul. The idea is that if something matters to someone else, it matters to me. I don't need to know why, but I have to help, comfort and get relief for the other person if possible.

In a family setting where personal love is best recognized through possessiveness, unconditional love or impersonal love is rarely understood or even desirable. The idea of "if that's what you want to do, of course, it's all right with me" began to be taken by others to mean, "She doesn't care." The gaps in the marriage widened. The intense feelings about some issues and the total freedom in others created too much confusion to be acceptable.

Another dilemma was to find a way to tell others that while I would sit in the calmness of meditation, another kind of life was unfolding. Recollections of people, scenes and times I didn't know consciously but that I recognized, began to occur. Then, fortunately, I found a book on reincarnation. Sorting through the logic of this philosophy, pieces of my own puzzling memories began to fall into place and order came to be the mosaic that was my life and my challenge.

Later a noted hypnotist came to talk to me about the pyschic field. He had an interest in psychism and especially in sensitive children. He questioned me about a number of areas and then asked me if I'd ever been really frightened or had a bad psychic experience.

I shared with him an experience I had at age 15. I was away from home in a boarding school. One night I had awakened from sleep seeing a beautiful lady in my room. With a Catholic background all I could think of were the stories of Lourdes, Fatima, etc. I was scared to death. Our Lady only appeared to saints and I knew I wasn't a saint. I closed my eyes and covered my head with the blankets.

Now years later under hypnosis, and after the soul exchange, I chose to explore this experience. I didn't know what would happen but my own curiosity was such that I entered into the experiment. This experience has since helped me better to understand the make-up of the personality and its tools.

As he led me back in time I felt memories sharpening as I experienced two, three years before. Time adjusted back to age 30, then 25, then age 20. I felt a bump in the memory and emotions as I shifted into the recorded data of the other Carol. The emotions were sharper, more guarded and fearful. Back to the experience of the vision of the beautiful lady who appeared. Before this moment I never remembered her speaking to me. Yet, as the question was asked, "Did she speak? Did she say who she was?" I remembered suddenly the sound of a gentle sweet voice saying, "I'm

Theresa and I want to help you. Your life is very hard. Offer yourself to me and I'll help you. There is a bond of love between us and I'll come to you whenever you call."

In the stunned and surprised state of Carol's mind, this had registered only on an unconscious level. Later, at age 19, Carol was confirmed and took "Theresa" as her confirmation name. Though there were six daughters and Theresa was a favorite name, Carol never gave it to any of the daughters born before I entered. To her it was special and reserved for something else.

I have wondered about this experience as I have contemplated the many pieces of the Walk-in puzzle. I, the present Carol, have a love of Theresa of Avila. I admire her strength and courage. As a mystic she's more admired as time goes by and some years ago in a discussion with Leroy Zemke regarding past lives I shared my feelings for St. Theresa. He suggested this may be someone I actually knew or by whom a life had been influenced.

I believe inner plane experiences* were to teach me a great deal. One time I found myself in another dimension. I was walking across a campus with many other persons walking around and toward the same building. It seemed to be a very pleasant afternoon. I was walking with a man I did not know in my everyday physical life, yet in the experience I knew him well. It seemed he had vouched for me and was sponsoring me in an important matter. I was walking with him behind a young man whom I knew in daily life as one of my students. The man walking ahead of us carried a pillow and it had a sword on it. We proceeded to a fine elegant building, much like a cathedral. We proceeded up the many steps and into the great hall.

The room was lovely, long and imposing. At the far end we moved up another set of steps to stand before a man in regal robes who was obviously the authority there. Ceremoniously he took the sword off the pillow and said, "Who

---

*An experience of another level that is remembered here, usually occurs behind the veil of sleep like a dream, but feels entirely different.

vouches for her?" The man by my side presented me. The wise one said, "Turn and look." And as I did, I could see out through the walls as if they were glass, yet from the outside you could not see in. I saw many persons going about their business.

Then he turned to me and said, "All those who have helped this one, take a step forward, and all those she has helped, take a step forward." I looked and I saw many who moved knowingly forward at his command. And, I also saw many take a step forward unknowingly or unconsciously while active in their own pursuits. He tenderly said to me, "Remember how interlocked we all are. No one gives to another without helping one's own self, although it is not always in one's mind." Next I was kneeling and he blessed me.

Some weeks later in Atlanta, I received a special gift. I was a guest in a lady's home while lecturing in the city and she invited me and some others for dinner. The door bell rang and I went to the door. One of the gentlemen standing there said, "Carol, do you know me?" "You are the man who was with me . . . there, aren't you?" I gasped. He took my hands and knelt down there in the entry hall and began to pray. Later, he said, "So seldom when we know each other on the other levels can we bring that down here and recognize each other." We laughed and hugged each other, much to the stunned looks of the bystanders. We shared our story and had an evening of getting acquainted. I have never seen him again. Only once I called him in an emergency and he told me, "Remember, Carol, the spiritual path is a jealous mistress. If you give yourself to it, you can have little else." A powerful truth, yet as we give ourselves first unto God, everything else shall be given unto us.

Another experience of great significance for me came in much the same fashion. I had another inner plane experience, I was in a lovely room in what I thought to be either Germany or Switzerland. There was a grand piano in the room, a superb chandelier and several rows of splendid upholstered chairs. The latter faced two grand windows through which one viewed two prominent magnificent mountains. A short handsome dark haired gentleman entered the room. I was on the front row. I knew he was a great man, a great teacher. I was thrilled to be there and to hear him.

About five years later, after I had discovered Agni Yoga and had located Torkom Saraydarian, I flew to California to meet with him. I found him in a large room and although it was different from the room in my inner plane experience something brought that other room into my mind. This room had large windows and I looked out as I walked to take his outstretched hands. Behind Rev. Saraydarian I saw two large mountains. He said, "It is nice to be with you again. I met you in Germany, did I not?" I stumbled out the words, "I have never been to Germany." Smilingly he said, "Now we know better than that, do we not?"

One must remember the goal of meditation is to develop the antakarana and to gain conscious knowledge of what is going on at each level or plane of one's nature. And if, in fact, we are beings both spiritual and physical, or both soul and personality, then we acknowledge that just as the personality lives the everyday mundane life, the soul lives a high and holy life. Then the time comes when we from the physical-material level, invite the soul-spiritual self to enter into the experience here. Prior to this, vast separations exist between our physical nature and our spiritual self. Spiritual hunger signals readiness for such integration and the quest begins.

Also we must be aware that behind sleep, our non-physical part is free to continue its activity. There are a great many stories of eastern masters and also western saints who have practiced bi-location: conscious awareness of being active as a personality and a soul. This kind of phenomena has attracted considerable attention as a way of proving, if we choose that term, that life exists in more than the simple process with which we are most familiar. Meditation is the bridge to the higher world and as we develop spiritual attributes many other kinds of awareness can come to us.

Chapter 6
Being A Student

Private lessons with Ann were supplemented with classes with other teachers. Eastern philosophy expanded my understanding of the similarities and differences existing between Christianity, Hinduism and Buddhism. Rev. McBride Panton of St. Petersburg guided me through Vedanta, Upanishads and the Bhagavad Gita. My horizons broadened again as I began classes at the Spiritual Center, a St. Petersburg center for the training and ordaining of ministers with classes for other interested persons. I had no idea of entering the ministry. I simply sought comfort for an insatiable spiritual hunger.

At the time I was a student at the Spiritual Center, Rev. Thelma Fischer and her husband, Rev. Elmer Fischer, were directors. These two had a fine reputation for their program. They had about seven excellent staff members and conducted a weekly public worship service as well. Rev. Irene Palmer became my instructor and polished my skills. Irene is a Capricorn, practical and down-to-earth and her effect upon my work continues to show. Her support of me and the constructive criticism she gave has served me well. Her words of wisdom I often hear as I work with young students to help them refine their impressions and make them meaningful. I have made the statement that Ann took me right into college level material. Certainly she stretched me, gave me glimpses of the beyond, answers to my big questions and gave me the overall picture. Irene gave me the basics, many how-to's. Here I sat in class and learned the foundation of kindergarten and grammar school. Gradually the two came together. Also, here at the Spiritual Center, a metaphysical version of the small Bible college, I began to publically lecture, learned to pray in public "spontaneous" prayers, and to give psychic messages. The Temple of the Living God and the Spiritual Center, both located in St. Petersburg, gave me nourishment while I lived in Dunedin with my family of small children, quite unaware of what was going on in the life of their unfolding mother. Now my heart goes out to my parents who watched and wondered what was going on with their hard-to-understand daughter. On one hand they knew I was struggling and searching, on the other they just wanted me to settle down and go on being their nice Catholic daughter and not to make such a big deal out of all this stuff they couldn't understand. The years strained them and yet they too saw the intense young woman become more joyful, free and happy.

These were wonderful years. My life was busy, happy. My inner nature rejoiced in the bliss I discovered as I entered into periods of quiet. I listened patiently to the guidance from within. I learned the meaning of "witness consciousness" and could observe myself in my struggle and in my folly. I began to realize there was Carol, a personality waking up to powerful potential, and another wiser level of Carol that moved into play when the occasion was right. This latter Carol felt freedom to believe in idealism and high principles often hard to bring about in everyday life. This one understood the challenges of human life from an impersonal level. She knew her vision held great reasons for beginning that could not yet be shared. Simple day by day duty was performed seriously and she waited for the path to become clear. Time passed, and as I became more ready for service, I found the two levels of my own nature more integrated.

In these years the outer personality went through all the metamorphosis needed to help me define values and to pare away all unnecessary responsibilities. A moving personal experience led me to seek ordination and to move from the business world into a position dedicated to help others in their spiritual search. It was 1971, the human potential movement was awakening and I found myself in one position after another offering my insights and helping other individuals as the surge of interest in sensitivity gained momentum.

Believing myself to be one who is committed to working with humanity for as long as it exists, I harbor no feelings of "let's hurry up and get it over with." Many persons express great grief or unhappiness being in physical form as had the young Carol. Many spiritual students long for "getting off the wheel" or "being freed from here." Others, especially if less philosophical in nature, dislike the idea of reincarnation because they dread being "re-cycled," as they put it. At the same time, we find many who find hope in reincarnation because they've found no satisfaction in traditional answers.

My position is that it is important to believe that because we're living here on Mother Earth, we have an opportunity. It matters that we see value in our sojourn here. First, we need to realize that the opportunity exists; we either respond to it or not. There is a basic question which the philosophy of all major religions seek to answer: Is there a reason to create a postive attitude about life when it is so often a difficult and/or tragic experience? Some religions answer suggesting the ideas of cycles and rhythms and cause and effect. In fact, this is the most common thought. The Christian scripture can be read to support both of these theories.

The familiar verses of Ecclesiastes, "To everything there is a season . . . a time to reap and a time to sow . . . a time of war and a time of peace . . .there is a time for every purpose and every work,"[7] help us to grasp the concept of the movement of cycles.

"For whatever a man soweth, that shall he also reap,"[8]

---

[7] King James Version, Holy Bible: Ecclesiastes 3.
[8] Ibid.; 11:1.

and "Cast your bread upon the water for you shall find it in many days,"[9] help us to understand the cause and effect.

We see spiritual aspirants encouraged to be of service to God and one another. Choosing between good and evil is often suggested as a major reason for life having been given to each of us. To witness is a frequent response. All of these responses challenge us to "live well" as full participants in a higher plan. To hate life, to dislike playing its games, is to give our opportunities less value than the Creator gives to the experience of life.

As we begin to believe there is purpose, we can generally see the opportunities at hand. We begin to realize hating ourselves and our bodies is self destructive. Not to like life throws us into conflict with the human self preservation instinct and can only feed elusive pain and distress while undermining our bodies as well as our emotional and mental health.

Often in esoteric circles, beings really grieving or unhappy with life are seen as foreigners to our system. If this is so, and I believe there is some truth to this, these persons are living out of synchronization with this time, so attuned to whatever was that a great deal of waste is occurring for these in the here and now.

If we can believe that we are here for a collective reason, if not for an individual purpose, we can take some steps toward realizing life more deeply. If we could study humans with the same insights we use in sensing other forms of nature, we would determine that humanity is learning how to use power or how to create or even how to live in peace with that which it has created.

If we can believe some souls are committed to continue working with humanity through its vicissitudes, we are entering into an understanding of Jesus' comment, "Lo, I am with you always, even unto the end of the age."[10]

As each of us deals with the purpose for human life (indi-

---

[9]Ibid., Galatians 6:7.

[10]New American Standard Bible: Matthew 28:20.

vidually and collectively), we may find within us something that desires to add to this world we are creating. Leaving the world a bit better than we found it has blessed both the world and the individual lives.

If we believe GOD, or collective consciousness, or group mind can unfold great potential through each of us growing a bit, we may have the needed incentive to try. If we believe humanity is shaping the destiny of planet earth, we merely have to decide how we wish to vote; refusing or accepting involvement.

Great thinkers have dealt with the many philosophical insights of this challenge since earliest times. Perhaps we sum it up by realizing the wonder we each experience when touched by someone who has truly made a meaningful contribution. In our times we have the models of Mother Theresa, Martin Luther King and Mahatma Gandhi, who in far different ways picked something they could do and did it.

If we have the vision to see the contribution we can make and begin that effort, we usually can feel the rightness of our actions and thus we can feel the needed supportive energy coming to us.

Spiritual teachings reveal that the major opportunities earth plane life provides are in regard to those expressions not found elsewhere in other dimensions. The use of physical bodies in health and strength, the use of spiritual-creative energy in the form of sexuality, and the use of energy-as-money give us plenty of challenge at earth plane dimension.

It can be said that in this dimension we work with our resources in dense form. Our body and basic nature work together to create our tool box of traits, skills, strengths and weaknesses. Our sexual nature adds spice through the power of attraction and repulsion. Especially in this part of our nature we learn the rules that remain a part of the higher dimensions. The grasping of positive and negative power as electrically and magnetically functioning even if not clear gets us started. Certainly discrimination is demanded if we are to express our sexual nature in a positive and constructive way.

Collective energy can be called power or force. It can be called money. These ideas are very similar. When we store up influence for use we say we have power. When we save our income we have money. Both are resources we have to learn how to use wisely. Regulating the flow of income and outgo requires the use of our will for we'll either selfishly waste and indulge today or we will fearfully horde for tomorrow. As we regulate the flow of energy we can create and regenerate. This is a divine attribute, "made in the image and likeness" of the Creator. We create our life. With greater understanding we create what we desire as we consciously become a co-creator with life. As these awarenesses become our reality, joy flows fully and our sense of belonging is built. Much of the unhappiness that people feel comes from resisting creativity. Even a party isn't much fun if we do not wish to go!

In the 70's expansion of consciousness was in; parapsychology became a popular pursuit. An air of sophistication surrounded metaphysical terminology. Numerous people became armchair Buddhists. Yet, under it all, there was a pulsating honest-to-goodness search, sincere and hopeful. Students filled classrooms as meditation approaches were taught by devotees of one path, then another. The glamor of things rumored and wished for was broadly spoken.

Both students of science and art learned to meditate and most had at least one experience their logical minds could not explain away. A personal experience of insight or revelation or meaningful fancy helped many to reach their own subconscious in some acceptable way and expand their lives. Fast on the heels of experiential techniques came biofeedback to preserve the new progress in a technical manner with which our "dial and gauge" society is most comfortable. Thousands discovered through Silva Mind Control they could know something about another that they didn't think could be known. Other courses gave

precious new tools for healing prayers and psychic attunements and dowsing became more than "water witching."

Just as there seemed to be no limit to the acceptance of
new ideas, the tide began to turn. ESP is commonplace,
disciplines have again become dull. However, idealism, nobility and purity, the most ancient of principles, have survived the clutter. Old terms, steadfast through all the
phases of expansion, are still present as the level of interest
recedes.

The vibrancy of expanded experience in the 60's and
70's now has its impact in the 80's as a new basic belief.
The words become more traditional. What real difference
does it make to say that "spiritual energy is sweeping the
earth" or to say the same thing in "the action of the holy
spirit?" Those sincere searchers of the 60's and 70's, now
ready and strengthened by their personal experiences, integrate scriptural messages with the work of the New Age.
We are challenged to put into practice our reality on the
physical plane. We have learned much about many things.
The bottom line is, can we alter the rapidly degenerating
quality of life into the vision we behold of love, acceptance
and brotherhood? Can we create the vision we behold of
peace and sharing? Do we believe the lion and lamb are to
lie down together? Now my inner voice says to me, "Take
these steps and reveal thyself. If you love me, do as I say."

Chapter 7

Sharing The Aurascope

Having been introduced to Ann Manser, seer, and the first teacher of esoteric material I ever encountered, I became a dedicated seeker. I've often said my goal was "to know everything to be perfect." Ann had struggled, even as I now did, with her love of the Church and the feelings of having grown beyond it. Yet she spoke reverently of the Church and its purpose. Her respectful approach helped me as I tried to hold onto the past with one hand and reach for the world beyond with the other.

As I stated earlier, Ann did a particular type of analysis in written form; she called it an aurascope. The aura is the recording of life in color that is perceivable about each person, animal, plant and living thing. It is believed this vibration records our thoughts, emotions and soul patterns as well as incoming and outgoing energies. The interpretation of the soul colors Ann found in the pattern of the aura spoke to her about the evolution and purpose of each soul. I was eager to see what such a study could tell me about myself and/or my purpose.

In June 1969, Ann did an aurascope for me and here I share some of it. The entire material is quite lengthy, so I have chosen the most pertinent to our purpose. The aurascope began with an explanation of the uniqueness of each aura.

> In each aura there is some quality, shade, tone or pattern unlike any other aura and it is for this reason that each aura becomes a precise signature of the personality it surrounds. It is a faithful record in light and color of the

life and personality from which it emanates and of which it is a perfect reflection.

Colors of your aura are a clear and wide medium shade of blue; a very dark shade of blue; another medium shade of blue that has a pronounced rattling sound in it; a medium shade of blue that is a most joyous surging color; a regular singing blue; a dark and troubled blue that heaves in long rollers like the ocean; a light pink; a deep violet shade; one bright orange; one strange shade of orange-pink; a cream color with little straight pins of rose color in the cream. This gives you eleven colors and brings your present living and your living for the past six years under the vibratory influence of this number in which the soul and intellect of an individual receive understanding and wisdom from the "Spirit of God," the Aura of God which fills all space, the Holy Ghost.

As I read these words the first time, I recalled the years of 1963 to 1969, and I felt, "Yes, this applies to me." I have had so many experiences and have sought help from God so often, and so often it has come. Certainly all the unexplainable experiences seemed to me to be from the Holy Spirit. The paper continued.

This number and letter, Lamed of the Hebrew alphabet, teach that man's difficulties are self-induced and thus does man become his own judge and his own hangman. How long you will stay under the influence of the number Eleven depends upon how rapidly you unfold in your studies of the Wisdom Teaching. You may move out of it into a higher number within the next five years . . . or you may stay longer.

Looking back I feel I can see how wonderfully my life moved between 1969 and 1974. I truly believe a door opened in '74 and I flew free. It was in late '73, December, in fact, that I began the first spiritual community I lived in and a whole new vista opened for me.

Your aura as a whole field of color is bright and sparkling like a spring morning after a rain. In fact, your aura reminds me of a shower of rain just past—it glitters and shimmers as if colored drops of water were hanging all through it. It trembles all the time; not in fear, not for any special reason except that it is your nature to be vibrant and alert, ready to move forward, ready to please, ready to improve in any way possible. All of your colors have one thing in common—they have a joyous uplifting vibration to them, deep within each color. No matter what happens to your outward material life, this joyousness, this bliss consciousness of your true being, remains intact, untouched. In this way, you can always go to your "own center of being" and obtain help when troubled. This is going to God, of course. Your own inner center is God, your contact with God, your understanding of Him. This is part of your own framework, your own pattern, this Heart Center of God within your personality.

My life had already given me a great many tests which had proven to me the truth of Ann's perception to me. I had often wondered why, since my wonderful experience of the Presence, I had not known the kind of despair the young Carol had before. I began to believe the new me could reach a level the earlier Carol could not. Exciting new ideas are introduced:

This proclaims you as being an old soul—if nothing else does! In fact, you belong to the oldest spiritual family incarnating upon earth at this time. I might mention here that as members of this ancient family from another planet incarnate, they are only fragments, that is, the incarnated part is only a fragment of the whole personality (soul). It is like taking a book off a shelf of books to study for a certain reason; you don't need the whole shelf of books, you only need just the one for this time. So you choose just the one part of your personality—a spirit-economy, you might call this, to be use in this one life at this one time. The rest of the personality is accessible as you learn how to approach it, how to raise your consciousness to contact it. When the time is right for you to do this, you will be able to do it.

This idea forms the basis of my understanding of the High Self or Christ Within and helps me to understand

that individuals may be focused at a lesser level while they
have much more "in their storehouse" waiting to be discovered. I also feel this makes it important that we realize
those precious moments when we get guidance from our
own higher self and not always be too quick to believe the
information comes from an outside source, guide or wise
one. Sometimes we need to realize it may be our own Self
waking up!

> *The Great Central Sun of your planet is Sirius. That is
> where you come from, to where you will return even-
> tually; your own spiritual home. As each one of us, who is
> incarnating, work with one attribute of the whole family,
> we often can get overloaded on one thing, but thus do we
> continue to purify and spiritualize that one aspect of the
> whole group.*

Here you hear my heart sing, as she tells me of my
spiritual family and ties!

> *Perfume of your aura is a "violet" fragrance, not violets
> themselves, but an essence scent of all violet flowers mix-
> ed together. It is a fresh and lovely fragrance, again like
> flowers that have just been washed in a spring shower. It
> would not surprise me to know that you weep easily and
> often . . . all these glowing rain drops in your aura!!!*

When I read this today, I think of the many persons especially in my work with my death and dying ministry with
whom I have cried. I also realize how easily in a close and
sentimental moment I can feel the water come into my
eyes. Often these tears are happy and joyful. It just seems
my cup runneth over.

The aurascope continues to describe each color and explain its meaning. We must remember Ann was an artist
and color was a vital way she perceived life and so she
placed much importance on the various shades and variations.

> *Your first blue is a clear color of a medium shade and
> the color extends to quite a wide area around you . . . is a
> field color . . . used for about everything you do. It is ex-*

ceedingly active, very bright and observant—very, very pleasant in meeting the public in a business way. This color is composed, reasonable, calm at all times, even if some of your other colors are kicking up a row within you. You overlay this color, covering your whole personality with it, until such times as you choose to remove its protective covering. This blue is efficient, trustworthy, faithful, both to youself and to any other person to whom you feel an obligation. This is, first and most important, a business color.

Your second color blue is dark. This is an intuitive color, wholly. This dark second blue guides the first blue a great deal in all that you do. You glance into this dark blue, as into a mirror, before you go to work with the first blue and in this dark blue you receive your directives for the moment, and for the next move. For inner guidance you depend very much on this dark second blue—it has never and will never let you down by betraying your trust in any way.

Ann later told me, this indigo color is the color of the psyche. A color that is hard to identify on the physical but a very powerful color in the inner world. Ann taught me how to use a bowl of water and ignite the inner eye in this way. Later I bought a crystal and played with it. The water, the crystal, a mirror can be used if we have this inner blue with which to work. This color is used by the personality at a lower level as "the higher reflects downward" its message. We perceive with this indigo or soul color.

The third blue, Ann says:

is interesting . . . due to the sound it emits. Any medium shade of blue is a mental quality used in everyday life . . . in habit, the routines . . . daily duties and problems. This blue sounds like teeth clicking together in a chill. The sound is audible to my objective senses! This is a kind of static nervousness you have fallen into by having too much to do, too much responsibility, by being rushed for time. . . . Actually you do have enough time. This blue has got into a habit of tension. . . . You are carrying a heavy load of responsibility by choice . . . as you chose . . .

*just before you came into it—you have your life well or-
dered and going along as you previously had planned. So
try to drop this tension. Rationalize about it. . . . Let it
alone to ride along as it is supposed to do. It will.*

*This third blue is a color of orderliness, precision, per-
fection—and a lot of things in your life, . . . want you to
think about these . . . perhaps you are putting too narrow
a view upon all three. Your whole plan of life is orderly,
precise—because you are following your spiritual direction . . . your plan is going exactly as it should. Isn't that
a type of perfection?*

*The fourth blue is the joyous spiritual color which bub-
bles over into your everyday hours of living. This blue
literally sings as it moves along. It is an acquisitive color
in that it spiritually knows there is a great deal of knowledge and wisdom you have not as yet brought into
demonstration in your life and it longs for this to come
about. As it longs and desires, it stays in this beautiful
bliss consciousness, this awareness of what is available
and of what will one day be yours. . . . Actually, this is a
mild state of samadhi, the heights of which all Children of
the Path desire to attain above all else . . . lovely color.*

Certainly these words rang true, as illogical as my life
had been I HAD been happy from some source within.

*Your fifth and last blue is a dark, stormy, surging color.
It heaves in great waves through your aura at times dar-
kening the whole field of color with its force and its
troubled appearance. This is your place of stress and
resistance in your personality, the repository within you
where all of the troubles and the stresses of your whole
spiritual family are placed along with your own stress
and strain. This is for you to overcome, to lift up, to sub-
limate. Whatever hits this place is put there for you to elevate. If something is there for you to work with, it is as if
someone came along and said, "Here, take this, too. It is
more of the same. You can clear both as easily as you can
clear your own. . . ." So you have both to work on and in
so doing you help the whole family advance in evolution.
Each member of the family has this communal thing to
deal with, both in the good . . . and in the adverse. When*

understood, it can become a most beautiful sharing, a kind of vicarious atonement, the highest place of brotherly love.

I have come to know this part of myself well. I now call this deep rolling wave of emotion "my Pisces part" when I feel it roll and dive into the deep sorrowful place. Somehow the painful depth of where that goes in its suffering and its martyrdom identifies with my Piscean ascendant and the Piscean Age we have just come through. With all this blue no wonder it had been my favorite color for so many years of my life. Later my favorite color would become violet, a strong second at this time.

Light pink is a vibrant color . . . smiling, gracious and attractive, with acceptable manners and mannerisms. Pink is a color difficult of attainment in an aura. It takes a very long time to get a pink . . . many lives of discipline, training in social behavior, training in ethics, in thinking of other people's comfort and well-being . . . after a long time this color and its attending qualities go inward . . . that individual becomes magnetic, naturally attractive and drawing, naturally attentive and gracious. People with this shade of pink are always pretty, beautiful, attractive if they are actually not, then they appear to be so, which is the same thing! The attained light from within shines through the physical form.

Violet, as a color, is a shade of beauty awareness, often a color of longing and nostalgic feelings about what one does not have and cannot seem to attain . . . it is a color of vision and idealism. Your violet is dark and rich looking, so there is a measure of contentment in this shade. Spiritually, mentally, and perhaps emotionally, you have attained beauty in your life. There is considerable healing in this color; not healing as a conscious going-forth attribute, but a natural healing force which comes from you as an intrinsic quality. . . . You will never do more with this color than it now is . . . it is as it should be for this life. In your next life following this one, you will use this violet in a much more important way. It will then be one of your most important colors in your that-life work, coming into its full force as healing and a creative color.

As I continue to grow and ponder the universe I wonder about the healing work of the future and feel intrigued by Ann's suggestion.

> *Orange is a color that comes easily before an audience. This is the color of the public speaker . . . an acort . . . an entertainer . . . an emcee. It is a color of the one to many . . . there is self-assurance in this orange, a kind of forgetfulness of self, and unself-consciousness. It is a committee color . . . mediator . . . an arbitrator. It never gets thrown off base . . . it never loses its centerpoint of thought. It can give out a "kidding" and take the same, without giving or taking offense. It is a friendly color, being quite certain that everyone likes it and you . . . and of course, that is the response!*

Whenever I find myself feeling terribly shy or vulnerable before a lecture begins, I have learned to visualize this color flowing to me and around me until I feel I catch its glow. Then I can feel the comfort it gives and I am ready to do my thing. I think the color awakens the Leo in my chart and helps in that way, or again it may be because it works with the lower chakra centers and that is where our sense of security resides.

> *Orange-pink is an unusual color . . . cannot be described because it cannot be pigmented . . . more of a psychic shade than a material . . . does not belong to our spectrum of color at all. This color comes from the Sirius spectrum and therefore does not mean what it would if we mixed orange and pink together. Here it becomes a mental prerequisite, a place in your mind where you do not think like anyone else at all. This ties in with your particular stress place and how you react to it. It is an inclusive color, as it operates in gathering together like vibrations. You cannot use it for yourself alone. You must use it for yourself as you relate to other people and as they respond to you. When other living beings require something special, you seldom try to figure out why they need what they do; you just take it for granted that what they require is the thing for them; that what they desire or what is the right thing for them to have (if you can obtain it for them). This is a*

wonderful selfless reaction. You do not like to be ques-
tioned as to why you want some certain thing when you
do. Let it suffice that you do want it . . . you grant the
same privilege to other beings . . . you help without impos-
ing your own will on others . . . this is one of the major
reasons you have been given this community-stress thing
to handle as regards your spiritual family. It never occurs
to you to say, "Well, what is he worried about THAT
for?" That he is worrying is the point! That is all you
need know to come to the rescue if you can.
   Cream color is even a color of sensitivity in an aura . . .
your cream is not given to getting your feelings hurt . . .
not that kind of sensitivity . . . this sensitivity of yours
goes to an intuitive understanding in relationships with
other living beings. Through this color you can immed-
iately put yourself in the place of another and see why he
acts and reacts as he does . . . through this cream, see the
action behind the result.

I have felt that both the orange-pink and the cream are
the vibrations I use in making spiritual attunements that
have to do with personality traits and the spiritual reasons
for why certain things had to be dealt with or what karmic
patterns were working out or what past life influences
(again spiritual) were responsible for what is happening in a
life. And the color study is drawing to a close.

   Rose colored pins, straight little pins with heads and
sharp point, are in the cream. A color within a color, or
super-imposed upon a basic color, has only to do with that
color. It is not related in any way to the other colors in the
aura. So your little sharp pins have only to do with what
the cream color exposes to you about other living beings,
what your sensitivity relates to you about them and their
actions and reflexes.
   Rose is the color of love. Pins are sharp and pene-
trating. They can hurt . . . when they are stuck into some-
thing, a situation, a problem, that comes to your atten-
tion, but even if you do inflict pain with the pins, they
eventually do good to the one upon whom you have used
them because they are motivated by love; always love; no-

thing else . . . kindness, compassion, love . . . backed by
your deep understanding, your intuitive understanding
and your sensitivity.

I cringe when I deal with all of this about my sticking
pink pins in others. I think I realize I do this. I have always
felt it very important that those who love us tell us the
truth; yet so often they will not. I see parent after parent
who cannot see clearly his child. I think we protect those
we love by believing them to be different than they really
are. I think if we can get clearer and clearer about who they
really are and still love them, we'd be happier and so would
they. If we could stand to hear the truth about us even if
delivered with a pin and still love others, we could clean up
our act and have the support we need. I say all of this as an
Aquarian that has to have criticism given to me in little
doses. I was told in my guidance to speak the truth in kindness. In that way I can also receive it. So, to those we love
it becomes more important that we do be truthful for both
their lives and our own.

All this color information has come out of the aurascope
Ann did for me those many years ago. I have withheld
some information thinking the real teaching material is
here for you. Her work was fine and very exacting as you
can tell, filled with detail. Here you hear some of my beginning clues of an identity with Sirius. Later some of the
astrological details will also call Sirius to our attention.

Ann was of the old school offering her ideas on a one-to-
one basis, mostly oral. She spent years writing though, to
preserve her ideas for others, and left the Shustah
Material* as a legacy for us. Ann's perspective of the Ancient Wisdom was primarily Christian Kabbalist. Her
writings include 66 lessons (12 to 18 pages each) on the
Wisdom teachings, and 66 lessons on the Kabballah. Since
color was her favorite media, "the work" abounds with the
theories of life . . . vibration . . . as told through color.

Ann explored the Evolutions thoroughly, as well. Her

---

*Pages of Shustah, 901 17th Ave. N.E., St. Petersburg, FL 33704.

perspective was that many streams of life, called families, were incarnating in our solar system. Earth is a "slow" planet; the human kingdom is excited and inspired by contact with others. These ideas are basic to most "gnostic" thought. She made it real to her students in her unique and colorful way.

I was offered the idea of being a soul incarnating from the Sirius family, of the Free Soul Evolution. I know a great many persons across the country have studied this material, so you might find this interesting to plug into those concepts.

It is heady stuff! I've often looked back and thought how fortunate I was that I had to go to work each day and struggle with "being in balance at the end of the day." It is said Pythagoras taught that unless one studied mathematics or science one shouldn't have access to wisdom teachings. He may have had something! My evenings were caught up in the raising of the children. During those years everyone was still home and though my high and lofty fantasies dreamed of devas, spacial beings and messengers from Sirius, dinner had to be cooked and the laundry waited to be done.

Today as I see this heavy work pattern and family demands built in the lives of impatient and fervent aspirants, I know it is a blessing of God, and if both the stretching of reality and the grounding in earthly effort last, in time a great soul will stand revealed.

Here we see clearly the challenge of the Walk-in, the would-be messenger. Can this one know he/she has come into this dimension to give a message, and while they stretch themselvees to deal with this powerful information, can they be of any earthly good? Many can.

Chapter 8

The Challenge Of Knowing Thyself

A helpful idea was presented graphically to me by Ann in one of our sessions when she told of two paths which are used to grow spiritually. She used the symbol of the Kaballistic Tree and said that I, as most spiritual teachers, am on the Arrow path, while humanity as a group consciousness is on the Lightning path. Let me show you:

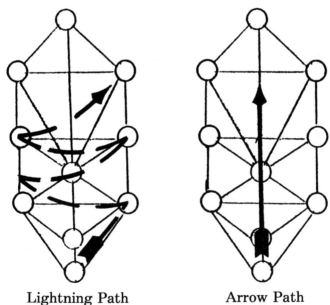

Lightning Path   Arrow Path

The Lightning path is always reaching for the balance as it is pulled by the polarities or dualities of the world about. One goes toward the mid-point, passes it, begins to go to an extreme, checks oneself or is checked by situations in the life and then again goes toward the mid-point. Walking the middle road path is a way we can see this process.

The teacher, usually fervent and in a hurry, chooses the Arrow path . . . straight to God, highly disciplined. These kinds of souls try everything, usually a great deal that is unwise, and they usually try to suggest the opposite to their students—not to try everything, to learn through their teacher's experience. The fervor of this "taking the gates of heaven by storm," type is powerful; the life dedicated and the energy focused into a tight pattern. This is how this type penetrates the secrets of the universe rapidly. We must then remember here the Kabballistic warning from the Talmud.

Kabballistic teachers taught: Four (persons) enter the studies. The first one died. The second wandered around and lost his reason. The third misused the knowledge and the fourth entered in peace and reached enlightenment.

The student of the Arrow path is considered in greater danger because of their fervor and lack of a natural balancing in the life as the Lightning path creates. With the move from one extreme to the other, as on the Lightning path, there is a slower progress, more balance and a gradual working to high consciousness. With the Arrow path, one can easily create fanaticism, imbalance and karma that will, in fact, slow one down greatly. The warning was really to say, "The path of a dedicated seeker and knower is fraught with danger." The teacher is a kind of protector for the student; but, the student has to be willing to practice obedience or the teacher can be of little help.

While this bombardment of data was entering my life from the outside, the inner doors continued to open and my personal life remained full. My business and professional life reached an exciting height; I thought I would be there forever. I felt strength and confidence. I held my own in challenging areas. Recognition encouraged me. I repeatedly saw the concepts I studied in private work effectively in the business setting. I used my perceptive skill to my advantage in the market place. Promotions came regularly; my income soared. I lectured as a personnel manager and utilized my understanding of personalities gleaned from my spiritual studies to build teaching techniques for team building and harmony in the office. Using these approaches the office I had joined cut its expensive and high turnover rate and this excellent firm solved its more serious staffing problems. And, of course, I loved it!

The inner life was equally exciting. I had struggled with finding a daily "quiet time" in a household that was never quiet. As a night person who could hardly get going in the morning I had settled on an 11:00 p.m. discipline time. By the late sixties, daily life began at 5:30 a.m., but no matter what else, at 11:00 p.m. I was home, quiet and ready for my meditation time. Ann, and then Irene, prescribed exercises and techniques for me to do. I wrote the impressions I received about myself and others in journals. I kept dream diaries and began to hear the wee small voice within self as it grew clearer. The uncontrollable waves of emotion or energy or both, of the earlier years, gradually came under control. I said affirmations and learned to talk myself "down" when I felt myself losing hold. I paid attention to diet and could see how sensitive my body was to certain foods and spices. Alcohol had never played a part in my life, nor had much meat . . . financially I had always had to be careful. I wondered if I had been protected. More and more I could see my existence, when things were necessarily simple, had served me well. I struggled with all the questions of sexuality as I found myself past 30, single and getting attention as never before for I had married at age 16, right out of high school.

Ann, Irene and Leroy listened while I talked. I gained some insight to my passionate nature that sought spiritual satisfaction. Ideas of celibacy fascinated me, especially in a society bombarded with sexual advertising. I was intensely interested in the restlessness of women everywhere. The women's movement was speaking to me. A tide of ideas and opportunities gave me places to explore and to share.

Women were inspiring me. I was deeply touched by the patience of Rev. Laurane Stroud, the founder of the Temple, when she told of her spiritual unfoldment fifty years before when there was no one who believed her in her experiences in Alabama. She was much more isolated than I had been. I was inspired by the patience women had in order to wait for their turn; I was impatient, wanting to get to it. I could see the stability women had, but still I chose to break out. I knew I didn't have that kind of time. I was turned off by the wildness of the early feminists and yet knew the time had come. I could not identify with some of the extremists in some ways, and yet, certainly could in others. I had suffered job discrimination and lower wages while I trained men for positions above me. I heard it said about me that men had to have more money than women because they were principal bread winners and I knew I had eight children at home to support. Strong feelings welled up and I knew the system was unfair. My parents understood when I argued with Life, but didn't want me to upset the apple cart for "those things have to move slowly."

I found I no longer could or would separate my spiritual concepts, my guidelines of life, from my office career. Everything merged into a challenge to make the world into a better place for me, my children, other women and yes, men, to live in. I felt "equality" is for the Soul not the body; there is no spiritual concept true unless it is for all . . . I had seen the wisdom of all religions and respected each one. I was comforted by the eastern teachings when I suffered from the logic and rational teachings of the west. I was angered by Christianity and its attitude of "this is the only way." I knew that if I had waited for the church to help me, I would have lost my sanity. I tried to subdue the anger, but it was even more apparent after my divorce and my loss of the Catholic support system, which would have stood by me through any abuse, but never divorce. My close friends evaporated by the scandal, although they had known for years my husband was involved with other women. It was a crazy system and fostered dishonesty, or so I saw it.

I craved freedom and needed spiritual food. I couldn't stand "pat" answers and yet wanted to know "what Truth really was." I wanted to know it all and now. The eastern teachings engaged my mind in wanderings that satisfied my searching inquiring questions and though they often only gave me more food with which to inquire, the koans also gave me peace. I, more and more, left the right/wrong perspective behind and found a new platform of understanding. I have said, a breakthrough came for me when I discovered "if one way is right, the other way isn't necessarily wrong." This was a powerful discovery for me. A real breakthrough for dealing with my guilt at not being like everyone else . . . I could be right, and others could be right. Their way could be right for them, and my way could be right for me. Hurrah!! I could now get on with being right with me.

Now I began to understand the impersonality with which I approach much of my understanding of persons is a way of being objective and clear with insights that I would lose if I were more closely identified or more personally centered. The feeling that I refer to is often spoken of as empathy rather than sympathy. So, I have been seen as aloof or distant. I remember one evening in the early seventies when Rev. Zemke took me aside and talked to me about someone calling me aloof. My feelings were so hurt. I remember saying to him, "But I care so much, how can it be seen as aloof?" He explained to me the positive and negative side of impersonality and how it causes some level of persons not to feel loved enough unless they too have learned to identify with spiritual love. My caring nature had much to learn about expressing that love in more open ways.

Each new experience gave me a fresh challenge. One Saturday, while doing my meditation, I will always remember. I felt this strong wave of energy move through my body. The physical body became rigid in response. I could hear a soft sound coming from my lips, almost a hum, when

I felt out of body rushing bliss . . . it seemed to soar and then it sort of burned down and settled in the head. My forehead pulsated with energy, I was somehow detached yet experiencing at the same time. The back of my head became involved and another circuit of energy was discovered. Then the top of the head itself seemed to be energized as well. The three points whirled with activity, expanding and rushing with vitality. As they continued to expand, suddenly my whole head seemed to be on fire with a new kind of experience. The three centers became as one functioning unit and then it passed and the energy settled into a small steady glow inside of my head . . . a kind of soft glow. Soon, a gentle inner knowing and stability began in my life in a new way.

A personality, formerly acutely sensitive and intense, began to stabilize. I could love others without overreacting. I could be more objective about my own personality weaknesses and began to really do some purification work.

The years of 1970-73 challenged me with strong ego, power struggles betwen myself and others, strengthening of all the weaknesses of my nature. Gradually and through the aid of the inner teacher, I was able to see more and more clearly these character flaws in myself and became willing to admit them and confront them one by one. It was not a "talking about" process. It was the down to earth doing something about these weak areas. Picking them out of myself one by one, I learned not to expect a short cut. I cried, prayed, apologized and mostly got honest with myself about me. I learned to shift into the inner part, find the Inner Guide and seek healing after each bitter struggle on the outer. The familiar sign of the unfolding peacock came to me again and again with words of wisdom. The tender words, of the inner voice, gave me hope that the spiritual fortitude would last and that I would live through the garbage. My ego, instead of being insecure became demanding. I experimented and found I could do most of the psychic games. I was tempted to the utmost. My fearfulness and my feelings of not having enough tortured me. It was a long time before I could turn loose of all the outer security aids and really give myself to the mission at hand. I bargained with God, giving in as little as possible, but gradually the life was ready. One day I knew that from now on, I would follow the guidance and let it take me to do that for which I had come. The resistance went out and I changed my lifestyle and my allegiance. But not until the most dramatic occurrence which I am now ready to share with you.

Chapter 9

My Secret Visitor

Often when a person reveals a remarkable story about the nature of an inner experience it is met with such incredulity that many keep silent, hiding these moments from misunderstanding minds. One such extraordinary experience occurred to me in early 1972. It was so remarkable and potent that I have guarded it as a gift beyond price, sharing it only rarely . . . until now.

In July, 1971, I had been ordained, and I felt I was very much upon my spiritual path. I had left my profesional employment and was beginning to teach spiritual classes and doing some private counseling. Also, I was associated with a local metaphysical church.

I lived in a rambling house and had a large bedroom which could be entered by either of two doors. One night, being alone and a bit uncomfortable, the last thing I did before getting into bed was to lock those two doors. I read awhile, as was my custom, and finally tired, I turned out the light. In this unusually silent and empty house I fell asleep.

Later in the night something awakened me and I became aware of the presence of someone else in the room. Incredibly, I was not frightened; the presence was familiar to me. I opened my eyes and, sitting on the bed next to mine, was a striking, tall gentleman, wearing Oriental attire. Dressed in an elegant robe with a turban of aqua blue silk on his head, he peered at me in a most serious manner.

Everything within me recognized him. I had no name to give him, but I KNEW he was not a stranger to me. I sat up and pushed myself back against the pillow. The scent of roses perfumed the room, although there were none present.

The gentleman said to me, "I am El Morya. I am the one who comes to you with the sign of the peacock. I have come to tell you many things. Take your pencil and pad and write down what I say, otherwise in the morning you will think this all a dream."

I reached for the yellow legal pad and pen I always kept beside the telephone and I began to write.

The message was profuse. My fingers raced to capture the words. His voice went on and on, calming, giving me information for which I had been waiting. As I wrote I questioned little of what was said. I obediently took down pages of material pertaining to my person and my life.

You are here for the purpose of God, the Plan and all others. You do not belong to your family or yourself.

Your home is to be a place of honesty and integrity. Your soul cannot live and do its work in deceit.

Your life is meant to be hard, because it has a purpose and much to be done before it is over.

Someday you'll look back and see where it has been five lives in one.

Your restlessness in regard to religion is because religion is mostly empty form. Your work is to revitalize the form into a container that has spiritual meaning.

As a woman you are asked to go where women rarely go and to practice bravery and courage. You are not to harbor anger or hatred.

Move forward through the lives you live without looking back. This will challenge you.

You are of the first ray on loan to ray two for a holy purpose. Healing is needed for the world. Aid all persons in a healing ministry.

The children are not for your happiness. They are tests for you as well as being loved ones. They care little for you or your work. Your influence will matter little to them. Do not seek pleasure here.

The world is your home, for it you will weep many tears. You are to love those unlovable and try to awaken them to their purpose in life. The love of which I speak is not emotional, but a rich supply of sustaining energy that flows into the life again and again. The supply is inexhaustible, but not everyone can understand this.

You are with me in another place and so you know me here. You will work with me later. Now I am awakening you to minor things so you'll be ready when the right time comes.

Whether I come again or not is of no importance, I have come once. It is begun. If you wait for me to come before you believe, I'll not come. If you do what I have asked you to, I do not need to come again.

My greeting to you is rejoice. Whether in pain or pleasure, in death or life, always rejoice. Rejoice that you have eyes and ears, that you have pain and joy. Rejoice that you are in your place doing that for which you entered in.

The carriers of the dispensation are few. Again and again you'll be blessed and strengthened by being in the presence of the spiritually great. This will cause joy and even sickness if you are out of synchronization with their rhythm.

You are to carry a harsh message. A message people will hate at times and many will misunderstand you. Does this stop one from being of the God? Angels treading among men must remember they are angels and not beg men to understand them. Do not cry out against those to whom you have come.

Your children provide you with an understanding of the weaknesses of the world. You need them. There must be heart ties to the human family.

Your students will reflect to you your strength. If you encourage, they will encourage you. If you doubt yourself, they will doubt you.

Resist not being a woman. DO NOT fear to break through the walls of restriction for this is part of what you are to do. Many strong and enlightened teachers from the past are taking bodies as women now to help bring in an equal age. Spirit can work in either equally well. Do not become a bitter woman, for this is worst of all.

My name is whispered daily in your ear—it comes to you to help you to grow wise and strong. For this you have come into this body.

I do not remember the end of the visit. The next morning as I awakened I immediately recalled my impressive and exciting "dream." I remained still, trying to pull details back to me. When I had grasped as much as I could, still in awe of the power of dreaming, I moved my feet to the side of the bed and behold!—there lay the legal pad covered with writing.

Quickly, I reached for it, and with shaking hands I read the dictated notes, some of which I have now shared with you. The enveloping feelings of rich love and the perfume of roses built again in the room as I remembered the visitor with the piercing eyes that had looked right through me to my soul.

The visit was real!! He had been here . . . in my room!!! Was it a physical manifestation or a vision? How could I know? Who was he? I had recognized him, but had anyone else ever seen him?

His clothes were so elegant; his manner so refined. His patience with me was in contrast to his piercing eyes. He seemed both tender and fierce. He had called me something affectionate, like "child." Later I came to know the word "chela" and later I came to know many other things about him.

This visit threw my life into high gear. I sought advice from Ann, Leroy and others. Everyone pointed me to the material of the Theosophical Society, Blavatsky and Alice Bailey . . . more doors opened. Leroy spent time, as did others, filling in the gaps of my understanding. I read everything I could get my hands on about the masters specifically, not just the term as I had related to it before. Before it was a rank, a level of development, a goal, as in the Masters of the Far East . . . now it was a person, most specifically, El Morya.

In my guidance another important message had emerged. Even before the visit of the master, from the inner self had come the words, "Agni Yoga is your way." Whether this was a telepathic thought given by another mind, or a deep insight from my own High Self, I do not know. Later, a writing in which the words are found again, "Agni Yoga is your way." The search was on. I had thought I was finished with the pursuit of the eastern way. I had chosen Christianity; I had been ordained into the Christian tradition and had made peace with the struggle of the church. I wanted to follow this way and believed it was right for me. Now, again I began to search for "Agni." To each eastern book or teacher I would ask, "What is Agni Yoga?" They would respond, "Agni means fire. It's not a way. It's a word."

I visited ashrams and teachers throughout the U.S. I opened the subject with each yoga teacher I discovered. They all knew the word, but there was no such discerned path called by name I was told again and again.

Then one day in a small booklet that mysteriously appeared on a table in my library at the Villa in Sarasota in 1977, I found the paragraph from *Hierarchy and the Plan:*[11]

> *In conclusion I will remind you that the yoga of the New Age will be the Yoga of Fire. The Agni Yoga, which will deal with the secrets of the Spiritual Triad and the technique of making the personality a pure channel for the expression of the divine fire within, the Spiritual Triad. The next step, then, will be to reach the essence of the human being, the inner fire which is his true Self.*

I was in the count down. I had found Agni Yoga. The

---

[11]*Hierarchy and the Plan*, Torkom Saraydarian (California: Aquarian Educational Group, 1975).

booklet was by Torkom Saraydarian, an Armenian born in Jordan. A thinker, profound and deep, who would stir my life for some years. I wrote a letter to Aquarian Educational Group of Agoura, California, and asked the wrong questions. I asked for information about Agni and they referred me to the Agni Yoga Society of New York City. I wrote there and asked for information on how to reach Mr. Saraydarian and they sent me back to Agoura and there I wrote to him. A letter quickly came back in Torkom's free-flowing open handwriting saying:

"It is so beautiful to know that people are working in the Light of the Lord. You want to tell me how you met M. M. and to be informed about Agni Yoga. I will be very glad to hear about it."

I jumped with joy when the letter came. I had connected with Agni and what to think about M. M. as well. I rushed for the telephone nad placed the call that was to take me to California to meet Torkom a few months later. Meanwhile, I ordered his books and devoured all I could find of Agni, which was not too much.

Through Torkom's *Science of Meditation* I read my first chapter on Agni. As I searched I found the name of a few other teachers. The word is still not used much. I have come to know Agni is a way and a technique rarely known as yoga. There are a couple of very hidden references in the Bailey material to the New Age approach offered called Agni, but so hidden it is hardly used by the Bailey readers themselves. I had, in fact, inquired of persons who were familiar with that approach in the past, but what can one say . . . "the time wasn't right yet!"

Agni Yoga challenged me in many ways and continues to. I am currently doing a lot of research in the subject and totally accept it as the New Age way. I don't think it will be offered in just the way most persons expect . . . but I see it growing and working in the lives of awakened ones everywhere. Many of these beautiful beings change and clear themselves through their fervor and vitality and do not have a particular name for what they are doing. Agni is subtle and since the word "yoga" is often unusual or uncomfortable for some, it is often entitled by Torkom and others, the Science of Ethical Living. Yes, it is now clear to me . . . Agni is my way.

I see myself actively at work as a part of the Christian tradition, a bit out on the fringe yet, but moving strongly into position to express leadership through understanding. I see the relationship between New Age teachings and esoteric Christianity. The time is coming for the revitalization of the Christian teaching through the integration of the esoteric understanding of the message of the Christ. The New Age understanding of the inner processes will help the awakening ones to have the spiritual life they seek and through the rediscovery of the knowledge of the early church, powerful changes will come.

We have reached the time in my unfolding story where I should point out to you that I was aware of a nagging pain in my life. I wanted to go to India. I couldn't get over my love of India. I had made peace time and time again with my western self and yet my heart was being pulled to go to India. What more did I want? I had an outer teacher who knows, I had an inner contact and inner teacher who had met my needs. What did I want from India? I didn't know. But I was certain that India was pulling me toward her.

Section III

Pilgrimage

Chapter 10

The Mystique Of India

I sat back in my seat as the plane took off for home. I closed my eyes and wondered if I would look different to people when I returned. I sat in the seat trying to recall how I had felt as I eagerly left for India. Had it been only two months ago when I had set out to fulfill my dream? It seems so long ago.

What had I gained from coming here? Adventure, for sure. New awareness; oh, so much. How can one put into words the encounters with the paradox of India: anguish, shock and then, the stunning beauty.

Only once had I really come apart. It was late in the afternoon. We were visiting a mosque when it came time for prayers and we hurried through the crowd of beggars to get on the bus. I was frightened by the men in the mosque who had started yelling at us. I recalled hearing about the beating of two western women in blue jeans in the Moslem section a few days earlier so I hurried the ladies with me, insisting we get back on the bus. This was our third day in Delhi and the pitiful sight of the beggars affected me so deeply. All the black-haired, black-eyed little children reminded me of my two-year-old granddaughter who had drowned only a month before I left home. Repeatedly, I found myself fighting back tears as I saw the pitiful little ones. I realized I was still dealing with my own grief and loss.

Sharp tapping on the half-open window beside me had caused me to whirl around and look. A frail girl, perhaps ten years old, grinned at me and held her mutilated hands up in my face. The fingers had been cut off at various joints. As she thrust her hands through the window at me, I screamed and burst into sobs. Grief consumed me. I buried my face in my lap and cried it out. As the others returned to the bus, I leaned back in the seat, my eyes closed, listening to the strange sounds, allowing the chatter of our group to help me adjust. Breathing deeply I calmed myself.

What a place of contrasts India is! Everything in human life is here and right up front. The most profound moments of quiet versus the constant sound of the hustling noise of human life. Great beauty, art and architecture is a backdrop for the ugliness of human squalor, filth and disease. India teaches because she is like ourselves . . . filled with every quality. The difference is that we tend to push away that which we do not wish to see. In our own culture we carefully learn to ignore that which is not to our liking. Here, in this great and profound place, with everything so new to us, everything to the extreme, we could not push away the bombardment of the senses. Data is thrust upon one from every side; sensory overload finally occurs allowing the next level of awareness to kick in and new objectivity to happen. I can't help but wonder if this isn't something like what happens when someone takes drugs. When one can't stand any more emotional pain, I have seen this happen. You move to another stage of awarenss. When a person jogs and the body can't take it, if he pushes on, the breakthrough point occurs, and suddenly he is no longer pressing the body, and there is the experience of breaking free. That is what coming here has been for me, breaking free at another place in myself. I get to be another me now, because here I went beyond what I had been capable of and found a new place, a new energy, a new knowingness. I now understand two things. The first, I have expanded the perimeters of myself a bit. I am stronger, more able to endure, less needy and more secure. Second, Babaji affirmed this newness in me. He gave me the touch needed to anchor the new found consciousness into my life.

When he touched me I realized the truth about what Ben* had told me years ago about "not yet having put my foot on my work path." In that frozen-in-eternity moment as I stood in front of Babaji and he put a lei of flowers around my neck, I realized with awe that when I moved my feet and took the next steps I would be beginning again. A next step had begun. For me this meant another time capsule in my life had ignited and the whole process of adjustment, processing, and becoming was back again.

Why did I have to think about it now? I want to be excited to be returning to my husband, family and friends. I am going home and I am going to try to share what has happened in these wonderous days.

My trip to India had begun in my mind about 1970 when I had been deeply touched by a home movie about Sai Baba, shown by Roy Eugene Davis.** I had studied eastern teachings, Vedanta, the Upanishads, the Vedas and enjoyed the philosophy. But the movie made me "homesick." I felt such a pull. That night I knew someday I would go "home to India," at least for a visit. It had taken ten years for the right time to come.

Ben Osborne went to India to travel alone for some months. When he returned, he helped plan a trip for me and several students. We made a list of all the places most importance for this once-in-a-lifetime dream.

Our trip was planned for September. The preceding May a magazine article was brought to my attention with the

---

*Ben Osborne, a young spiritual teacher located at Jasper, GA, and close friend.

**I had been drawn to Roy after I learned he had studied with Yogananda. Once during my meditation I had had an image of a holy Being in front of me. When I glimpsed him in my inner eye, I had been filled with peace. This great peace seemed like recognition and wholeness. It drew me into close communion and led me to study more and more the eastern way. I later found a copy of *Autobiography of a Yogi*. In it I found the picture of the being who had appeared to me. The book called him Babaji and introduces him to the Western world. I determined that if Roy was of that lineage, it would be to him I would go. I was initiated into Kriya and settled into practice. The breathing exercises caused me trouble. I found myself returning from unconsciousness time and time again. I finally gave up the technique, but never the relationship to the tradition.

question, "Have you ever heard of this guru?" My eyes
scanned the page. "BABAJI is in body again. BABAJI can
be seen in India. BABAJI has a body and is seeing people."
My mind reels. This is why I am going to India. I sat down
and read the lengthy magazine article. I quickly write a
note to the author, but my whole being was still. I know
this is where I am going. I whisper the name "Babaji" and
feel that great peace. Yes, Babaji knows I am coming to India. I can sense it deep inside me. Perhaps I have been
called, I do not know. All that matters is that I will get to
see him.

Just in the way it should, the response comes. The
ashram writes to us to come for a visit. In September we
are on our way. The large group is traveling together for
most of the trip, but for a brief week, I and four others from
Sarasota will slip away and go to Babaji. What will he be
like?

I had left home battered and bruised by the deaths of
my daughter and granddaughter in August, just weeks
before. Some persons suggested that I should not go
because of this. However, I felt that the trip was especially
going to be appropriate after those terrible weeks. It would
be a time to get well and to deal with the loss and grief. I
said my good-byes to Karen, my sixteen-year-old, and
thought how young, pretty and precious she was to me. I
kissed Charles good-bye and kidded him because of the article about life in Babaji's ashram. "Don't you act surprised if I come back with my head shaved. Don't bat an
eye." I wondered inside, "Would Babaji ask us to do that?"

Ten of us toured England, exploring the cathedrals and
the ruins . . . contemplating whether or not Jesus lived at
Glastonbury. Did our Lord of the Christian tradition live
here and have we lost that information? Titern Abbey,
Stonehenge, etc., brought new insights every day. All too
soon our days there were over and those of us who were going on to India rendezvoused with Ben at the London airport. "At last I am going to India. I AM GOING FOR
SOMETHING SPECIAL. I CAN FEEL IT."

Chapter 11

Sunrise On The Ganges

We were only half way to India when we got our first surprise. Flying on the Air India Jet suddenly two MIG Jets pull up alongside our plane. A lengthy message is given over the public address system . . . in Hindi; then a one sentence explanation in English. War has broken out between Iran and Iraq and the air corridors over those countries have been closed. We are being escorted to Kuwait while details of a new flight plan can be negotiated. A strained hush silences the plane. We look at one another. It is almost an hour before our plane taxies to the far end of the runway, where it is surrounded by armed Arab soldiers. We sit in the hot afternoon desert sun while the plan becomes increasingly uncomfortable. Babies cry. The tenseness of the situation is revealed in the tone of voices. At last, three and a half hours later the word comes, "The plane will be serviced, refueled and we will be on our way to Delhi." The service crew enters and carries off our litter. They refill the water tanks and I remember the Indian flight attendant saying, "Don't drink the water." Soon we are on our way! Looking back I can see the symbol of the trip . . . confrontation and change of plans, requiring us to keep the faith . . . if we could!

I was unprepared for the airport at which we arrived. The babel of so many tongues, the eyes peering at us from the glass enclosed balcony above. A sea of brown faces, and each one saying something in a tongue I couldn't understand. Our plane is six hours late now. Exhaustion has long since numbed us. Our tour guides locate us and bring us through customs and the crowd to a waiting bus. It is a typically Indian bus, years old and held together with hopes and wishes. The friendly hired host begins to give us his tourist guide spiel as we are driven to the hotel. Stunned, we look at the countryside. Dawn is just beginning to break. It is a nightmare. People are sleeping in the street, beds by the side of the road. People squatting and eating by tiny fires. Bicycles, cattle and water buffalo vie with us for the road. The calls of the birds are so loud, the smells are so strong. The ride begins to be a blur of agony, do I look? Can I not look?

Checking into the hotel becomes a lengthy chore as we begin to find out how slow and tedious the paperwork is in India. At last the fourteen of us are registered and after getting situated in our room, we shower and are ready for breakfast. After being up all night we go down to breakfast and find an antique, slightly musty huge dining room. The table is set and breakfast, fried eggs all ready, waits on our plates, long since prepared.

I had wanted my first outing to be to Mahatma Gandhi memorial gardens. Ben had engaged the guide to take us out at 9 a.m. for our trip to the gardens and the eternal flame. We gladly finish our meal and push on to the outing to visit the spot where Mahatma Ghandi's ashes are preserved. As I place flowers on the memorial I am overcome with appreciation for such a man as he. How can a great soul as this be truly appreciated? Dear God, bless this one so wise, so gentle and so strong.

Only today is the movie "Gandhi" being released. Through it, the public may understand the work of such a mystic as he. The power of the vision he carried led a country to freedom without a shot being fired. Can the world realize what a great spiritual influence this one carried to have accomplished so much? What kind of change can we create if we could live in such a dedicated way? Such possibilities could be realized if we hold his example in our mind.

From here we begin to visit the temples. Everything seems so vivid; the colors so bright, the sounds so loud. All seems so primitive, so shocking. Buildings are badly crumbling. Hot. (Dear Heavens) is it hot! The guides say it is approximately 105 degrees. The monsoons are just over so the humidity is making it hotter, and the tourist season is just beginning. Often the hair of the children is bleached red on top by the sun. I am shocked by the wild boars and pigs rooting through the streets and along the roads.

Bike riders are everywhere, clogging the streets in a traffic pattern I have never seen before. There is a disorderly rush of trucks, cars, buses, bicycles, as well as a wagon here and there, clamoring for the right of way. Whoever makes the most noise seems to win. As our bus rushes full speed ahead horn blaring, I often close my eyes convinced we're going to mangle others in our path.

The shrines are beautiful from a distance but lose their charm close up. We visit Embassy Row and I am thankful the U.S. embassy is subdued. The country of Kuwait has a fine building and I gladly remember our involvement with them. Thank goodness these two governments seem to get on together. Most hotels and public buildings look tattered and torn from the outside, like old elementary schools. The banks are like stale notary offices. One bank guard had a stopper-like something on the end of his gun. Like a toy soldier, so proudly he stood.

All the confusion seems to be left behind a few days later when we visit Agra and the Taj Mahal. As I step through the door of the wall, with my first glimpse I have the familiar feeling of wanting to genuflect. The beauty impelled me; I felt like a fish being reeled in, immersed in complete and holy silence. I moved without effort toward the magnificent form of the building rising before me.

I remember as a child I had cut out the picture of the Taj from a vacation Bible school magazine of my grandmother's and pasted it on my wall. I told her it was the most beautiful cathedral in the world. She patiently explained it wasn't a church at all, that it was a tomb. However, any place I encounter such beauty still seems like a cathedral to me. I walked quietly down the long walk to the

Taj, climbed the steps and entered in. Hearing the voice of the local guide explaining the building and its history, I fought the emotion of such beauty. Later that night the group went back to have the full moon meditation of Libra on the grounds. Afterwards, as we sat watching the mist rise from the river behind, I realized that, yes, I had come home to India. For what, I didn't know yet. But I knew this was for me. The day after our visit to the Taj, we pushed on the Varnasi, another place of wonder for me.

Varnasi, the holy city of the Hindus, is often called the City of Death. Here each Hindu prays to come at leat once in his lifetime. The fervent desire to bathe in the River Ganges pulls pilgrims from all over India to its banks. So, too, it has pulled me. For a long time I have wanted to be in this reverent spot at sunrise!

Now I am making the trip through pre-dawn hours. The dark ride in a bicycle rickshaw jostles me, as the human body pumping the pedals in front breathes hard, pulling me forward. Noisy birds and other strange sounds float in the air. It is exotic and I thrill with anticipation, filling with delight in it all.

As we proceed through the darkness I begin to distin-guish distant temple bells and chants offered to strange gods with strange names. The language is shrill and scary. Shadows move about, come close, then pass, filling the air with the sound of labored breathing. In the pre-dawn light I notice the shirt on the back of the small dark man in front of me becoming speckled with sweat. The phrase, "By the sweat of the brow" comes to my mind as I ride behind him.

Shadowy forms standing still are soon passed by. I glance at the bodies lying along the side of the road. Al-ready the smoke of morning fires fill the nostrils as people begin to stir. Men squat to toilet on either side of the road-way as the rickshaw crawls on. The Ganges is our goal. We must be there before the sun comes up.

Five miles or more we have covered, barely escaping the bumps of cow and truck. We turn to a narrow path . . . always to a more narrow path. Finally, we stop, and I must leave the rickshaw and walk. This street is so narrow I could stretch my arms and nearly touch each side. Here, close to my destination, tiny old people patiently squat. More noise reaches my ears; a child cries. Flower vendors already are in place. The river waits.

Persons are coming from every doorway as life descends to the Ganges. We go to the steps, quiet now; silent as the unborn. Deep in our own worlds, with closed eyelids we wait. Crying, weeping, remembering, breathing, we wait. Then, the guide calls softly, "The sun, she comes." Opening my eyes I see dawn's first signal and the warmth touches my heart.

I turn to the river; it is silver on silver, cool and passive. Moving slowly and silently, it looks like shiny, thick mud; the darker silver silhouetting the lighter. All life seems to wait.

As the sun's warm pink glow begins its upward movement it kisses the shimmering buildings. Ascending the heavens this fresh stream of light holds a straight line. In full view, its glorious color expands outward to gold. Now the silver river becomes golden. The stream of gold in the sky meets the stream of gold across the water . . . and we wait.

For a time, only the birds dare to disturb this place. Then, movement, as a limping widow comes to pay her call. Her flowers fall into the water and she sets aside her cane. Slowly, gently, she enters into the golden mud-water and begins her morning bath. "Mother River, Mother River, I am ready. Release me. Release me. I am ready," calls her chanting plea.

I notice her wet garment hangs on bone and little else. Her hands roll and unroll the wet cloth; the ritual takes care of itself as she smiles at the sun. Finishing, she crawls to the edge and stands, wrapping herself in her other rag, sliding the dry over the wet. Deftly, swift of hand she is done. Gathering up her incense urn, her bag, her rag, her lot, she begins to climb the stairs.

I am watching. The press of the crowd affects me. I

move in slow motion as in a dream. The beauty, the
strangeness, the chanting voices calling to God, seem
unreal. It's very dramatic here. Life and death bump into
one another every minute. An old man breathes a deep sigh
and in the next moment he is done. A beggar moans, a
donkey brays, a child cries. I am about to weep from the
crush of this open exposure to raw life. At this moment my
attention is caught by the boats sliding so easily over the
water and I become detached as my heart glides with them.
The pain, the fervor in my heart rests. My heart opens
and expands in its quest for understanding. In this place,
at this time, in this ritual of all life coming to the sunrise, I
learn.

I reach into the water with my cup. Pouring the water
over my head, my need to come to the River of Things Ancient has been met. Now I smile, ready to move on into the
present. I feel the deep bond of the human search and I rejoice in a sense of oneness with all life beginning this new
day.

"Let there be Light. Dear God, let the light come on
more strongly within me," I send my prayer heavenward.

In the next weeks we visit Bodh Gaya, Gaya and Sar-
nath. We visit the Park of Buddha at Bodh Gaya where we
entered the temple to see the huge Golden Buddha, clothed
in orange cloth waiting to greet us. The gilded statue sat
there, flowers everywhere about it. We were welcomed in
by the monk, stepping barefooted about the floor we stepped on the coins left there by others. We sit silently for
awhile and then go outside to climb to the second floor. We
walk about the roof on a high narrow temple porch. Here
our heads are in the leaves of the Bo tree. I picked a leaf to
press. Here is the slab where Gautama Buddha sat. Coming down the steps, walking the grounds of the temple, ad-
miring the railings (the wall carved with characters and
symbols to preserve the teachings of Buddha that King
Asoka had erected), I realize I am standing on the soil on
which Buddha walked. I feel every bit the pilgrim I know
myself to be.

We walk under the trees and to the Lotus pond where Buddha centuries before had washed. We go down the steps and silently and reverently wash our bare and dusty feet. The pond is at the bottom of a grassy slope where teachers sit and talk. Special devotions are going on now for departed parents; so many others are around and about. Mantras are being said by the crowd; first the priest and then the people respond. As I listen I am reminded of the Mass for the dead.

We chant, look, pray and contemplate. We sleep in the government rest house and awaken many times each night to the call of holy men as they chant to the god they understand. We survive energy shortages. The temperatures are well over 100 degrees and the electricity is in short supply. So while the fan hangs silently in the ceilings we understand in a new way the real meaning of "no energy, no electric." At night we use candlelight for dinner and dressing and swelter in a land where an electric fan is a luxury. Yes, we are learning. A Buddhist monk kindly talking to us one day said, "Buddha gave a great commission even as Jesus did. He told his devotees to 'go now and preach the doctrine to the masses'." The monk states, "Two great masters ruled with compassion . . . Buddha and Jesus." Everywhere in this setting we are reminded of Buddha's message to mankind, "If thou wouldst worship in the noblest way, bring flowers in thy hand. Their names are these: Contentment, Peace and Justice."

From here we visit the school of Swami Dwarko Sundrani at Gaya, which we have been contributing to for some years. The good Swami in memory of his wife, who died giving birth to their first child, a girl, began a school for the poor girl babies being thrown away to die or forced to beg and suffer all their lives. The swami collects the children, educates them, pays a monthly stipend to their families in return for giving him the little girls so they need not help support their families. After the children are raised, Swami Sundrani has the responsibility of finding husbands and dowries for each.

Today he has gathered together the group of 20 to 25 little girls, 6 to 12 years old, to sing some Hindi songs for us. After three or so songs, he then tells us the little girls have prepared a special song in English for us for all our help. They begin to sing "We Shall Overcome." As they sing in their clear young voices tears run down my cheeks. The memory of my beautiful blond daughter and her small brown-eyed baby comes to me. The deep pain of death seem so close here as life is lived so openly. Yet here is what it is all about. One step at a time, one human at a time doing what he or she can do. Peace comes to me as their little voices give me hope.

From Gaya we flew to Nepal and Katmandu with all its Nepalese temples, art and mystique. The land is cool, comfortable and clean. The population is smaller and the food is better. A week here to rest, browse in the art shops, ride in the countryside prepares us for another month in India. As we prepare to go back we excitedly think of Babaji. From here we fly to Delhi. Then we'll leave the others and trek off to the hinterland to meet him. We are frightened to go so far, just the five of us. Yet, this is the big moment for which we have come.

India, as I see it with unaccustomed eyes, looks like a lovely, gracefully shaped silver dish with most of the silver worn thin. The design, the patterns are carved, but the finish has just worn off. It is an antique country, beautiful, but has had daily use. There has been no repair or maintenance of the buildings, no major replacements, no new inventiveness since the British left. The fervor of new independence is here, but the barreness of hard human living is making itself felt. Buildings have not been painted for years. Any new buildings are of brick and plaster, often unpainted. The glamor of a rich past exists, as evidence in its "has been" state. There is no feeling of vitality; no feeling of expansion. There are too many needs to determine what is the one thing to do right now. Too much philosophy preventing India from getting on with the tough business of progress. Yes, I do think like a westerner!

Chapter 12
Off To See Babaji

In Delhi I am scheduled to lecture for the Indian Federation of United Nations Association. A special friend and former member of parliament, Savtri Nigram, now National President of the Indian Housewives Federation, has arranged a gala evening. Many politicians and influential individuals are there and I am invited to the palace to meet Premier Indira Gandhi. Of course, I am delighted. On the following day we do just that. Also, a very helpful gentleman introduces himself. He is the manager of the Imperial Hotel where we are staying. He offers us extra service and assistance. After the lecture I go meet with him and share my anxiety about five ladies traveling alone.

His kindness and offers of help are genuine. He calms my concerns and asks me to tell him how long I need a driver and car and he'll guarantee our safety. We rest in his assistance as he arranges the details. We are going to be gone over a week. He even stores our extra luggage as we scale down to a minimum. We study the map and find the town named Haldwani, at the foothills of the Himalayas. Tomorrow after our visit to the palace we'll be off.

Before I had left the USA, I had received a letter from Babaji's ashram* giving us permission to come to Herak-

---

*To write Babaji:
   Babaji, Shrishri 10008 SVHRI, Bagwan Herakhan
   Watebaba, P.O. Herakhan, Vishva Mahadham
   via Kathgodam, Dist. Nainital, U.P. India 263126

Organization now formed in California to distribute information in U.S.:
   Herakhan Samaj
   1304 Woodside Road
   Redwood City, CA 94061

han. Upon my arrival in India, I had to find out where
Haldwani was. The directions received are uniquely Indian
and can give you a feel for the travelers far afield.

> *His Holiness Shri Babaji has received your letter and he
> sends his blessings to you.*

> *You are welcome to come to Herakhan to worship at his
> Divine feet.*

> *To reach Herakhan you should take a bus from New Delhi
> to Haldwani—in Haldwani you should go to the Kailash
> View Hotel where the manager will assist you to reach
> Herakhan.*

> *It is necessary to bring a sleeping bag, a wok and your
> own plate and glass. . . . Women should equip themselves
> with a sari and a bathing suit (not bikini).*

> *It is also necessary to change money in New Delhi as it is
> not possible to change foreign currency here.*

> *We also recommend the repetition of the holy mantra of
> Shri Babaji: Om Namah Shivaya (I take refuge in Lord
> Shiva) which will help you as a preparation for meeting
> the Great Master.*

> *With best wishes.*

With a map of India we found the small town of Haldwani. After the six-hour train ride from Varnasi to Bodh
Gaya we realized we couldn't handle the bus so we rented a
car and hired a driver. This is a much more comfortable
way to travel and is possible for less expense than ima-
gined.

We left the city behind. Our driver spoke very little
English and we struggled to communicate. A handsome
sikh (an East Indian religion) with a stately manner, we
often wondered if behind his solemn manner he was
laughing at those strange American ladies who stopped the
car to take pictures of huge vultures, water buffalo and
naked children.

Travel for women gets increasingly difficult due to lack
of bathroom facilities. Men relieve themselves anywhere; it

would appear women never need to. A subtle way to keep women home is to culturally avoid public rest rooms and consider it forbidden for women to toilet in public. Rest room facilities exist in the lovely western hotels which are scattered sparsely through the larger cities. In the countryside some cafes and public buildings (airports and train depots) provide opportunities for relief. Travel is extremely difficult under any conditions.

At one place our driver located a cafe with an outdoor garden area for us to have "Limca," a popular lime drink. Of major importance was a clean rest room, a small room with a faucet and a hole in the floor. We stood in line to enter one at a time. Being so far from the path that travelers usually frequent we were such an attraction that a huge crowd soon gathered to watch us stand outside the bathroom. Afterwards, as we left the enclosed garden, we discovered some 200 or more persons gathered to look. Being the only blue-eyed person in our group, several times I was touched to cause me to turn and look. Then people would point at my eyes and grin. A friendly people those Indians, openly curious and eager to make friends. While the beggars and poverty was shocking, the instant acceptance and open affection of everyone encouraged us. Everywhere we enjoyed our contacts with individuals as we and they tried to bridge our communication gaps.

Upon our arrival at Haldwani, a lengthy train blocked the highway. An eager school boy rode his bike over to the car window. He stared openly right into my face. The air was hot and dry. We had traveled six hours or so and were slightly giddy and delighted to be close to our destination. I spoke to him, "Hello. How are you?" He let out a squeal. He replied, "Hello. My name is _____." He again said something in barely understandable English. He whipped out his school composition book and showed me his writing. I began to read his pages. He grinned from ear to ear. He said he had never spoken with "an English" before. I said, "We are Americans." The train soon moved and we could go but again a crowd had gathered and a few wonderful moments had been shared. The young boy gleaming with joy, stood and excitedly discussed our interaction with his peers.

We were soon able to find our way to the Kailash View Hotel. The sign was in Hindi so we ladies were really uncomfortable when we arrived. We communicated so poorly with our driver that we weren't sure this dilapidated building was our correct destination. No one was in sight as we drove through the low walled enclosure. The driver stopped and everyone sat. I earned my medal for bravery when I got out and began to call for someone. No response. I wandered around. It was now dusk and we were increasingly uncomfortable. I walked through a gate and found myself in a court yard. An old man was stirring a pot of food cooking over an open fire with a stick. Again I spoke. Carefully he turned around and began a flow of Hindi words. I shook my head and said, "Manager, please." He shook his head, "No." My heart sank. Again I began, "I am looking for the manager. He is expecting us. I had written him from New Delhi. Manager, please." He had gone back to stirring his pot.

Suddenly from behind me comes a commanding voice speaking in King's English, "What can I do for you? What do you want?" Whirling around I am delighted. "Yet his manner was distant and cool. I begin again, "The manager, please. He is expecting me and my friends. My name is Carol Parrish. Are you the manager?" His response was, "What do you want? What is your business here?" Feeling very much at the end of my rope, I asked, "Is this the Kailash View Hotel? I have a letter here giving me directions to the hotel." "What is your business?" he asks again. Now I respond, "I am to see Babaji. The directions are from him."

Instant success! The gentleman in a grey striped western suit breaks into smiles, bows from the waist. I said the magic word. He shakes my hand, apologizes for rudeness and yells at the old man in Hindi, who now gets to his feet with full attention!

We proceed to the car to get the others. Fearfully they have waited for me to reemerge; our driver never moved. He has brought us to the destination. The blessing in disguise is Mr. Shrivastava who arrived earlier in the afternoon with the news Babaji is coming here in two days. Mr. Shrivastava becomes our instant friend and confidant. He takes it upon himself to care for us and to introduce us to rural India and the inner Hindu culture.

After seeing the dinner stirred with a stick, cooking outside I decline for all of us when asked if we wanted to eat. We asked for hot chi (tea). We had bought bananas and apples on the road and a whole loaf of wheat bread. We scrubbed the fruit with Basic H and ate in our room. Peanut butter wisely brought from the U.S. became our staple and we settled in. We were told we were being put in Babaji's room. We were honored. Yet to us the quarters were almost primitive. We very fortunately rejoiced in a bathroom. It was small, with the faucet just off the floor and the usual hole. The entire area sloped into a drain in the center of the room. Here we bathed, did our laundry and used the toilet . . . luxury, Indian style. We were glad. Later in the evening we became aware our quarters were shared with a large furry creature, a jumbo size rat. Only two of us saw him and didn't tell the others. Things are hard enough as it is.

From my diary I share my notes. "I look at my inner feelings and ask why the master or masters are hidden here? Does Indian know what is hidden in these mountains among these people? I ask Mr. Shrivastava, who says, 'No. Not .001% of the people know anything. They think it is a fakir's game.' He talked of the OM and God setting all into motion and his firm belief that Babaji, Himself, is God. Here we are in the Himalayan mountains in a glorified hut, scared, excited, out of touch with our world and our realities, hearing exciting miraculous tales of God. We get ready for a night's sleep in a room we are told Babaji uses when traveling here. A fan works softly overhead as we place a cover sheet over a board bed. The bed is made of

strips of board with a little cotton coverlet on that for a
mattress. We take cotton sheets out of our pack. We save
the sleeping bag for cover when the night becomes cold.
We are international searchers . . . blessed, frightened and
growing."

I lie on the uncomfortable bed beside one of the women
and together we ponder what Babaji will be like. I wonder
to myself if I can see through the surface of such culture
and find the holiness of any one here. Could I see the light
of God in such circumstances?

The eternal struggle is to see the light wherever it flows.
How can I avoid letting the childishness of others capture
my attention in such a way that I fail to be receptive to the
joy, love and divine power which are also present. I realize
I do not need to say anything particularly to him. If he can
see my love and my pain, he will know and respond. If he is
divine, he'll know. If he isn't, he doesn't need to know. If he
knows at a deep level, I think I'll see it in his eyes, or voice,
or words. If he knows it at another level and I already am
believing this is so, he will let me know if I need to know . . .
I think I can understand this. So much struggle to wonder
what others understand. Why do I have to struggle for acceptance even here? Why am I asking myself this . . . I
have already had so many insights . . . why do I require
another?

How does one go to meet a guru? "Free yourself from
expectations" come the words from inside. The expectations will block the flow of grace. Be receptive to what
happens. Do not anticipate what will possibly be going on.
Just be here and now. Feel. Know the cultural patterns and
try to accommodate them. Let there be as little resistance
as possible. Remember, rules are structures to try to help
us know what to do, so try to be comfortable. If we can
remember this, we can "resist not" the guidelines.

Why such respect for the guru? The Christ within
should have and give respect to every living thing. We
learn to increase that respect usually through status
games. True respect for saints comes from realizing how

hard life is, how hard for us to perform. We respect the effort that they have made in their own patterns. If one is able to give of himself in so many ways, and so openly to so many, who are we to judge? Give respect, because the one we watch helps to draw others nearer to the God force within. The spiritual teacher struggles to grow and guide at the same time. We are all on our individual path. Some teacher may throw light on our particular path and we can give thanks. Can we receive what is offered to us by being in their presence? Our big question for now . . . can we be receptive to the grace of a great being in a setting so strange and uncomfortable for us?

This we will soon find out. Several times today we have had opportunities to observe new beings and new ways. We have prayed and cried, struggling to understand, and have had both fears and joy visited upon us. We seem to know this special one will ignite our struggle even more. I remember the teachings of Leadbeater in *Masters on the Path* regarding placing yourself in the presence of a great one. You can now see your own imperfection more clearly. The great Light or Aura pointed directly at ourself shows to us the weak areas of our nature. Our unfinished effort will be activated, our uncleanliness, or unpolished parts will be illumined, enlarged so we can see them better. Yes, this is why we have come here. This is why we are so uncomfortable at times.

The next morning comes early. Three a.m. sounds awaken us and get us started. The cold baths taken by the faucet only 18 inches off the floor take time. The night is very cold from the mountain air. We must bathe, wash our hair and be ready for meditation by 4 a.m. We understand little of what is said to us except "today you will meet Babaji. You are so blessed he comes to you." Yes, this we know. We have waited for this day!

At last the guide comes to us and says Shri Ramesh is ready to go meet Babaji. We can go to the mountain or we can wait here. There is no question, we will go to the mountain. Little do we understand what is meant. Later we'll laugh about our ignorance but now we are just anxious.

Our first moment of meeting was on the mountain trail. The jeep raced along the trails climbing an ever steeper, narrowing path. Our small, hired tourist car rushed along trying to keep up. Our driver was good or we wouldn't be here to tell the story. None of us were quite sure why we were the only ones following the jeep with Sri Ramesh and his driver. We assumed it was because we had the only vehicle but the jeep only had two people in it and it could have held two more. Everyone at the Hotel Kailash seemed to have much to do. The ashram set up in Haldwani was about a block away and a festive air was everywhere.

When asked if we were ready to go meet Babaji we immediately answered, "Yes," and Sri Ramesh got our driver. The adventure began. We had no idea how far we were going. I truly thought we'd make a mistake after an hour's drive, going higher and higher in the mountains. We followed the jeep having left the hotel staff and guests behind, getting ready for their Guru. Was the jeep really going to meet him or going somewhere else? We didn't really know.

Each of us have been challenged by these strange days. One woman, always so picture pretty, is trying to keep her hair nice. Another's depression is long past now and she is cautious, but taking more and more part in the activities, finding her inner strength and trying to reserve judgment. She catches herself judging, checking, erasing and struggling. A third woman, being most new to the group, is far more egotistical. She is trying not to be so forward. She had handled well Mr. Shrivastava's remarks regarding her ego. When we first met, this was his way of being protective and helpful, hoping to spare her a public reprimand later. None of us enjoy the dirt, the discomfort and the confusion. We have dressed carefully preparing ourselves inside and out for the day. Wrapped in white muslin saris, one step removed from bedsheets, none of us are beauty queens. However, we truly feel we paid our dues for this occasion.

Custom is, we had been told, the first time you meet a guru you present yourself in white. Not knowing this until Delhi, there we outfitted ourselves in simple white muslin saris. Our sleeping on board beds and living in different kinds of quarters, no mirrors, peculiar food, etc. has taken a great deal of starch out of our sails. Mr. Shrivastava has spent two days with us "getting us ready." He has filled us with wonder and steeped us in Indian mysticism and tales of Shiva, Brahma and Vishnu. Our heads are swimming.

We have been taught etiquette by Mr. Shrivastava. He has told us how to enter the room, to bow, to present gifts, how to eat, etc. He has taken a special pride in getting us ready. His love for Babaji is expressed in many ways. He speaks of his family's relationship to Babaji and how his sons feel. He dreams of years of serving him in the future.

The trek up the mountainside becomes scary. We look down off the edge of the narrow trail at what appears to be thousands of feet. The deserted trail, always becoming more narrow, commands our total attention. In the front seat on the right hand side is the driver with me beside him. In the rear seat are the other four women. The small car is very full.

Suddenly on the trail we round a curve and meet a truck decorated in Indian style, adorned with trinkets, pictures, statues and leis. People sit four abreast in the front seat, we can see a half dozen or more in the back standing up and looking over the cab. Just as suddenly the jeep is thrown into reverse and begins to back down the hill and around the mountain. Our driver follows likewise and I close my eyes. Finally the trail widens enough for our driver to back off. The jeep backs by and the truck passes us to come to a stop. Sri Ramesh and companion jump out of the jeep and run with armloads of flowers to the truck. Now we realize Babaji is in the vehicle! This is what we've come for. Our driver does not move. Sri Ramesh gives no sign. The truck roars off down the mountainside, the jeep races to keep up and we swing into the line.

Where did the people come from? All along the sides of

the mountain trail people are lined up shouting, waving palm fronds, throwing flowers before the truck. Out of the jungle along the trail have gathered the mountain people. We had traveled this path only minutes before. Not a person was visible; we thought the mountain path was deserted. Where did they come from? How did they know Babaji was coming this way? I couldn't help but think of Master Jesus and his triumphant entry to Jerusalem.

As the trail reached the paved mountain road it widened. The truck stops and so does the caravan. We sat in the car and watched a figure clad in green silk disembark. Another figure ran to the stream and returned with water to pour over the tall person's hands. From the distance we could see someone hand him a towel. Then he turned and walked directly to us. As he approached I thought, "Is this a man or a woman?" So gracefully the figure moves toward us. Then he stood beside the car. As he approached, our driver had opened the door and fell at his feet. Babaji pushed the door almost closed and stood looking at us.

All the preparation and good manners taught by Mr. Shrivastava were forgotten. We looked into the face. Even as I write this today my heart responds to the memory of such love. To describe the eyes, the face is beyond words. His eyes examined me. I felt hot tears pouring down my face as he looked. His eyes explored the inner as well as the outer. With the piercing scrutiny of the Indian people he didn't mind staring. His eyes were brown, clear and filled with love. I remember thinking, "I bet Jesus' eyes were like this . . . such compassion and complete understanding." As he continued to look deep into me I remembered my manners and placing my hands together in prayer pose, bowed from the waist as deeply as I could, seated in the confines of the car. His eyes left me and began their examination of each person in the back seat. He gave the same lengthy review to each. When finished he smiled warmly, spoke in Hindi to his two companions who had stood waiting close behind. He spoke to our driver, waved and returned to the truck. Someone spoke from the back seat, "Why did we cry?" I suddenly realized each of us had experienced such a rush of feeling, tears were flowing down every cheek.

Our driver was joy-filled. His English was so limited we had hardly been able to communicate even with patient effort. Now it was useless. He babbled with joy. He had seen Babaji before, he told us. He loved him. Baba had touched him. He would serve us forever. Babaji had accepted us, he said. The driver promised he would take care of us. He poured out a lavish display of respect and love.

We followed the truck, completely caught up in the drama occurring before our eyes. It would stop and pick up someone. Greetings were returned. Flowers were everywhere. Women held up babies. Men and boys shouted, bowed and waved. The driver picked the path slowly down the mountain. Triumphantly we were going back to Haldwani to the ashram prepared for Babaji.

Staying in an ashram in the U.S. or India helps one to recover from a great deal of glamor. Certainly our experiences of joy and love in any group are real and when abroad the cultural aspects do add charm. But the required hours of remaining seated challenge me. I find the hours tiring after the new wears off and my active nature begins to get restless. Having experienced ashrams in America, I found the atmosphere of the Indian ashram little different, although Babaji himself kept me enthralled.

To describe Babaji's face is challenging. Day after day he presents different aspects. Sometime I looked at him and realized an hour later how much he had visibly changed. His face reflects the room, the people, the feelings or mood that is about him. Sometimes he is young, sometimes he appears old. Yet, there is no gray in his hair, no lines on his face. He is always aware of his audience. He watches them, their behavior and their moods. He amuses them, plays with them, accepts their love in a peculair and unique way. At moments I would see a fleeting sadness move across him. He held an elderly woman tenderly one morning, kidding her until she hid her face and then he

sang to her. The business of the day goes on before
everyone. People go up, and after bowing in the appropriate manner, ask questions, receive blessings, have
babies blessed and converse. At times persons came to him
to settle quarrels and to solve family problems. They bring
letters for him to see and discuss business matters. The
setting reminded me of a day in the life of a king and his
court. For all life here in the small village turns on his word.
He calmed people and reprimanded them. He took time out
to teach a bit; then he called up persons from the audience
and gave shakti.* We watched amazed and bewildered. I
realized I wouldn't want to stay here long. A wonderful
place to visit, but I wouldn't relish living in this environment all the time. I have to find my own way in another
culture. Babaji knew we were struggling; he let us struggle, watching. He sent us goodies to eat as he tossed smiles
and love across the room. Playfully at times he'd call someone forward, talk to them, smile and joke.

---

*Eastern term for spiritual power; feminine; holy spirit. Gurus direct their
energy to devotees to cleanse and awaken the holy spirit as an aid to the
devotees' life. Example: slaying in the spirit or the leaping of the spirit from one
to another under inspiration.

Chapter 13

The Blessing Itself

Upon entering the room whenever Babaji sits, custom is for one to go before him and bow. He usually sits on a kind of backless couch. One bows, touching one's head either to the couch just in front of him or to the floor if desired. One day, upon entering the room and respectfully bowing, Babaji took my hand and said to me, "You know where you live is not safe." I heard myself calmly responding, "Yes, I know." The truth is, I didn't consciously know it or at least I didn't want to know. Charles and my life is good . . . better than that, it is great!

We live in Sarasota, Florida. For sixteen years Charles has handled the financial affairs for New College, responsible for budgets, personnel, purchasing, computers, buildings and grounds. (This experience would prove to be essential, as you will read in the last section of this book.) We had renovated a beautiful old Mediterranean style apartment building and had created an atmosphere of peace and healing. Beautiful gardens and a banyan tree, par excellance, graced the yard. A second building served as administrative offices, chapel, classroom, etc. Our needs were being met . . . nicely. I do not want to think of change.

Ever since I've been in spiritual study I have heard of the challenges expected in the latter part of the century. I've read Edgar Cayce. I've read of the earthquakes expected, weather changes and even the idea of the possibility of a pole shift. But not wanting to face the issue I had avoided "negative" subjects. Now, I hear myself responding to Babaji, "Yes, I know." I find my way to a spot to-

Sarasota

VILLA SERENA

ward the rear of the room where I go to sit. Aware of my tallness among the small Indian ladies, I choose to sit in the very back so as not to block anyone's view of Babaji. Chants are being sung when a devotee with shaved head and orange sari comes to me and says, "Babaji wants swami to talk to you." "Am I to bring my friends?" She replies, "If you wish."

We gather ourselves together and are led to an adjoining room where a white haired gentleman in the orange robe of a swami is seated. He wants to share Babaji's ideas with us. He says that Babaji has asked him to tell us many things. He will teach us for many hours. He proceeds to tell of God incarnating as man—always near the Herakhan country. Of Babaji's creating a body, yes, manifesting a body vehicle in 1970 to teach again and to be with his people during the end of the Kali Yuga, which we are in now. The stories become more and more miraculous. He says, "Do you know Jesus the Christ came to the Himalayas before he began his public ministry?" Yes, we know and so we proceed.

Babaji is supposed to have revealed many things to this devotees about the challenges just ahead. He is preparing those who come to see him to live simply, to love clearly and to hold themselves in a state of goodness and grace in these trying times. I sit there and listen. A part of me thinks, "I already know this." Another part doesn't feel too much in touch with it all. I remember thinking that "things seem real or unreal here because everything is so different. I can't trust my judgment here because of the culture shock. I'll think about this again after I go home. Now is not the time." Swami proceeds to tell stories of miraculous happenings of God, legends of Hindu teachings in broken English so we often don't know when he means Babaji and when the story is of another great saint. We spend hours listening to talks of future happenings, devastated humanity and the coming struggle between darkness and light. I realize how similar good and evil, light and darkness, salvation and sin are in every culture and each religion. I was glad when the Swami sent us back into the sanctuary with Babaji.

I sat in my seat with my eyes closed, getting centered, finding a place of peace within myself. Don't try to understand anything . . . just be, I thought. Suddenly a voice spoke to me inside my head. My eyes flew open. It had said, "Look at me." My eyes hadn't opened in obedience but in surprise. He was smiling at me. I looked away, closed my eyes in total confusion. Again the voice came, "Look at me." Carefully I opened my eyes. He winked at me and smiled. Later he spoke again, and when I opened my eyes, he playfully tossed an apple to me. Once he said, "Look at the door. A woman with a child is going to come in through the door." The windowless courtyard had no outside view. In a moment the door opened and a mother carrying an infant entered. From time to time, for the next two days he'd demonstrate this telepathic ability to me.

Babaji's teachings are particularly simple and clear. He carefully says to us time and time again, with the help of both interpreters and the swami he assigned to teach us, to remember the things one must do to live a spiritual life.

He implores all to:

1) "Treat all others as God."
2) "Feel empathy for others."
3) "Know all have God in them."
4) "Serve those about you even
   as you would serve God."

"Do these things. Do these things daily. Let your work be your meditation. Do not be lazy; do not shirk duty. Meditate briefly; work hard. Love all others as God." I asked him, does one have to do Kriya? He said, "No, any way you love God and keep the name of God on your lips is fine. Just keep the love of God in your heart and on your lips always. My way is a Universal way. Love God your way."

On the last morning we were to be with him, Babaji told us to be at meditation by 4 a.m. We arrived 15 minutes early, yet everything seemed to be in full swing by the time we entered. Torches were in place around the wall. The courtyard was two-thirds unroofed with about one-third covered. The women were in the more protected area with the men in the more open-to-the-weather part. The night air was cool, our shawls and saris were held close about us as we sat and chanted. The fire ceremony was done with each person brushing himself with smoke from the incense. Several trays of paschad (blessed treats in bite-size pieces) were distributed. A festive air was created. The drums beat and the peculiar music of India swept us along in the way of the east. Then it was quiet. The only sound was the gentle sound of breath. The people are so close, so many in such a small space. The American women, as we are known, are in the very back of the room. We are less comfortable with the long periods of sitting and wiggle more than the others. We try not to be distracting to the small, quiet and patient Indian ladies about us. We settle down, not quite sure just how to get up and down in our saris. There is always the feeling of one wrong pull and everything's lost. We have settled down in the deep quiet. Time passes slowly. The breathing seems to be in rhythm when the voice speaks in my head, "Come up here." I open my eyes in shock. There he sits eyes shut and quiet. I close my eyes. Again the voice says, "Come up here." I keep my eyes really shut now. I wait and I don't hear a sound. A third time the inner voice speaks, "Come up here." I think I'm going to cry. I can't move without disturbing others. There is no aisle. We're sitting a solid mass across the room. I take a deep breath and open my eyes. Babaji looks at me and smiles. I begin to stir trying to be careful of those about me. I try to stand. As I get to my feet, the ladies in front of me seem to evaporate to create a path leading to where Baba sits in front. As I look at him he stands and I begin to move slowly to him. As I get almost to him I go down Hindu fasion and touch my forehead to his feet. He reaches down and helps me get to my feet. Tears are in my eyes. The room is breathlessly quiet. He begins to speak in Hindi. He takes the garlands of flowers off himself and puts them around my neck. He blesses me, speaking gently. He says, "I bless you and I bless those you bless." He says more in Hindi to the people. The conch shell is blown. The room explodes in sound. The peple begin to yell, "Bhole Baba Ki Jai! Ki Jai!"

My years of studying astrology kick in and in the midst of the yelling and chanting and jumping up and down I look at my watch to see what time it is.* My mind seems detached and fully alert. He touches me again, smiles warmly, turns and is followed by his devotees as he files out of the room.

---

*See Section V, Event Chart #2, Oct. 9, 1980, 5:50 a.m. Haldwani, India, pg. 191.

The Indians are in delight. They are jumping up and down, chanting, yelling and touching me. My head says, "It's all going to be new now. This is a new beginning. A next stage has started." As I take the next step I begin my work path, as Ben has predicted years earlier. As I consciously explored these thoughts, I picked up my feet and took myself back toward my friends. In the medley of sound and excitement Babaji had left the ashram to travel elsewhere. Our driver, now indeed respectful, sees to our every need with fresh enthusiasm.

With an understanding of the East and the concept of Shiva made clear to us we realized evermore clearly the approaching of the end of an age or a time. Babaji dwells on the ideas of duty, love, clarity and ethical living. He pushes people to settle the past, do service, love others and heal their lives. Settle old debts. Be ready, he says.

All of these ideas are present also in Christianity and in New Age teachings. Recent channeled materials as well as the study of ancient traditions of our own native American people warn of a closure period. The fundamental approach to Christianity speaks of a great time of tribulation approaching. The message of ending and the struggle for new beginning is everywhere if one is courageous enough to look.

For me, standing and being blessed by Babaji was an ending. I could feel the connection made. His love surrounded me and strengthened me. Those days created a space between what had been and what was to be. I particularly became aware of a new understanding of the word Grace. It seems to be the right word for Babaji. It streams from him to others and it affects each in a different way. All of us were deeply touched. When we tried to put into words what had happened we realized how differently we were blessed inwardly. I had observed levels of myself ignited in different ways. When I really began to realize how much we each had received from him I could also see we grew according to our own ability to receive. He was to us a reflection of whatever we could perceive at the moment.

As I left the ashram, traveling back to the city I realized my heart was singing. The heavy sense of loss I had carried was no longer there. I felt bouyant. I didn't know where or how I would proceed but I realized a door had closed and a next stage begun.

I think Babaji's blessing was goodbye to my particular fascination with the East. I believe I am to go on my own path of blending and bridging, not looking back to the glamors of what was. The energy flowing from Him was compassionate. He spoke simply of doing what needs to be done, now. Build no illusions of the future, he challenges.

Chapter 14

Satha Sai Baba

It was Satha Sai Baba who first awakened me to India and I could not have gone there without visiting him. We were told he was traveling back and forth between Puttaparti and Whitefield. He was engaged in talks with government officials and there would be no private appointments possible. Hearing this, Ben and I had begun immediately to send Baba thoughts, "We are coming." Later, as our time drew close we began to send our mental message, "Come to Whitefield." Joyfully, joyfully, we prayed and hoped and worked telepathically.

We arrived at Banglore at 7 a.m. from Bombay. We reached our West End Hotel and were just settling down to breakfast when the manager brought the mssage Sai Baba had arrived the previous night at Whitefield. He would have darshan (a time of devotion where the guru gives blessing) at 9 a.m. That was in half an hour. We left our meal and rushed for cabs. Our hearts sang. We were heard!

"Indian time" is a joke to all those who have been there. This time it saved us. We arrived, found our places among the many, knelt and sought to calm our excitement before the palace gates opened and the cluster of individuals began to walk toward the small pavillion which shelters us from the hot sun. In the midst of a half dozen men clothed in white, walking toward us is a small delicate figure I know to be Satha Sai Baba. Familiar with his picture, I delight in being in his presence. As he walks among his people, taking prayer requests, blessing and touching others, our eyes meet and hold. I feel his gaze. I know he knows we are there. The atmosphere about Sai Baba crackles with energy. He carries an intensity that any sensitive would easily detect. His face shows strength and assertiveness. He strives to move people ahead, to awaken them to make progress, NOW. The energy is a surprise. Here is not peace, love and softness, but power of a new sort. The aura about him is filled with excitement. The power of his soul makes itself felt like generators humming along. I smile inwardly as I think to myself, no wonder he can manifest objects. As our eyes touch I felt I detected humor behind his serious demeanor and I thought, "How great he is." He knows all of this is God's great game. Even though he goes through a lot of hullabalu, he is really not trapped in the ego of it all.

Our days in Bangalore rushed by. We go to the ashram morning and evening for darshan. Each session lasts about three quarters of an hour and consists of the same procedure. We visit the bookstore, copy the thought for the day, engage in conversation with other devotees and compare notes. Rumors abound on ashram grounds in all of India. Communication is so poor whether in a city, sitting under a tree or the ashram grounds, news rifts like a breeze across the enclosures. Crowds gather quickly and explore every possibility adding more glamor with each statement. No one wanted Baba to leave and no one officially knew how long he was to be there so each day fed rumors and elevated the anxiety of those wanting to see him or to be touched.

Having heard the tales of many regarding Sai Baba, I knew one of the most customary stories regarding him. Time and time again someone returning to America had told of not seeing him or going unnoticed until their last day there. Then Baba acknowledges them and notes their departure. The story is old and hardly needs telling again. Yet, each day as we joined the devotions he greeted none of us, ten in number at this time. He picked his way among the men and the women blessing, talking and touching . . . never any of us.

The last morning we went to the ashram. Rumors were that he was leaving today. Many stayed around, hoping for another glimpse of him if he drove off the grounds. We purchased some books and admired the beauty of the spectacular Indian architrecure. Satha Sai Baba is recognized for the way he pushes his people. He approaches his work with the world in a more western and intellectual and achieving attitude than is usual for the eastern guru. He demands quiet and respect, refuses the adulation most gurus cultivate, and has standards less devotional and more actively oriented. He has campaigned for education in a major way. He speaks for equality of the sexes and works with the government in a modern approach for social action. His innovative approach has brought him much criticism from among the more traditionally minded Indians. I see in him an activist, a change agent, an individual not content with the spiritual mystical tradition but one highly desirous of achieving a thrust forward for his country and his people. The power of the personality is readily noted by both those who love him and those who are uncomfortable with his ideas.

As the morning was gone, we returned to the hotel. Our plane departs at 6:45 p.m. We swim the pool of the luxury hotel. We pack our luggage and talk about going home. At 2:00 p.m. we meet and discuss timing. There seems to be no way we can go to the ashram again and make our plane. At 4 p.m. I decide I am going one more time. I mention it to the others. Three of them decide they, too, want to try it. We leave our luggage secure and get a cab and depart eagerly. Was Baba still there or has he gone? The front row kneeling positions are taken by the early comers. We separate, three women and one man, to find places in the crowd to kneel. No two of us are together. An Indian lady on the front row beckons to me and gives me her place. Thanking her, I begin to settle down. I hold some beads in my hand. I settle myself and quietly say my "good byes" to Sai Baba and to India. I thank God for such a trip, such a shocking exposure to life and for the opportunity of being

in the presence of the many holy ones I had recognized and
the many I had not known. My heart is full, happy and settled. I say thank you to Babaji high in the mountains and a
thank you to Sai Baba for this place of learning. I feel we
have been heard because of the recognition I saw in his
eyes the first day there and because he came to Whitefield
after our prayerful telepathic messages. Suddenly, excitement stirs in the people and Baba comes. He walks across
the clearing surrounded by the swamis. He goes straight to
a woman in our group. He speaks to her in English, blesses
her and moves through the crowd. In a minute he places his
hand over the second of our women. Again he has acknowledged those on their last day. I smile and think, "thank
you." He crosses over and visits various men on the other
side of the pavillion. Then he comes directly to me. He
speaks and blesses me, touching my head, the beads, and
as I bow he reaches down smilingly and pulls aside his skirt
to place his foot directly out to me. I'm overwhelmed. I
touch my head to his foot. He speaks softly and I feel his
friendship, his well wishes and the power of his being. His
eyes are smiling and pleasant. I feel charged with energy
when he moves to the other pilgrims.

Darshan is soon over. We gather together, overwhelmed
by the wonders yet unfolding about us. We turn our eyes to
the palace and say goodbye before literally running for the
gate and our cab. We collapse into emotion inside the vehicle. We have connected with Baba! Wait until we tell the
others! Baba has done it again. The ride to the airport is a
happy blur. We're going home! We're going home!

What have I gotten from my trip? Certain serious awa-
kenings. I realize how truly western I am. I love the East,
have learned from the East, but now know even more clearly that I am a Western seeker. The teachings of spiritual
thought run so deep, motivated from the subconscious of
the daily lives of the Indians, that it shows in all they do. I
would like to see spiritual philosophy as interwoven into all
the aspects of western life as it is there. I appreciate so
much the remnants of the rich culture India had at one

time. I am overwhelmed at how fast the cultural growth
and achievement can decline when a society does so. Remembering the beauty of India 600 years ago, it is hard to
reconcile it with the problems of today.

The eastern spiritual life that is idolized by the westerner is rarely to be found and life in an ashram isn't as
blissful as expected. In a greater realization of myself and
my work for the future I shall work even harder to restore
the western tradition of enlightenment. I believe the West
is ready and able. The light of wisdom began in the East,
but now hangs high in the western heaven. We must use
our opportunity well. We are so richly blessed and our time
is nigh.

I wonder what happens to a soul who is born to the
opportunities most American's enjoy. If there is a law of
cause and effect, what happens to people who have so
much and appreciate so little. When most of the world
labors to get fed, what happens when one wastes every
day? What about souls with time to learn and serve and express, and yet they choose to desecrate the goodness and
opportunities almost daily? Yes, now I begin to remember
why it was I wanted to live, to teach and to be here now.

Love floods me as the plane rushes through the night
taking me toward home. I can feel expanded insights
pulsating through me. I take out my pen and write. Now I
am able to comprehend the meaning of Christ with more
body and fullness than ever before.

In the Kaballistic tradition there is a system of breaking
a word down and meditating on each letter. And so, I
worked with the idea of Christ in that way. The body and
fullness of the meaning of the word CHRIST reveals itself
anew.

C   for the moving *Charisma* of the dancing holy spirit,
    the fire that makes itself felt.

H   is for the *Hope* and the open presence of God easily
    felt as it springs into the heart, abounding full in the
    presence. Hope of expansion to be one with the great
    hope of the world.

R   *Reassurance* of the struggle to be in the presence of
the carrier of light is worth all of the pain and effort it
requires. Required effort realized, brings reassurance
at another level and peace flows to the lower part of
our nature.

I   the words *"I am that I am"* are felt, known and
comprehended in a new way inside my being.

S   the *Stream* of current that stirs, the living *Spirit*
merging into one happening . . . the spirit, divine, full,
arches the current within my being and stimulates the
desire to become one. The steady sustaining stimulation of cleansing moves through me.

T   Now is the *Time* for the fullness of self. Tender and
gently I allow, at this time, the outer world to be . . . I
think of nothing. I am completely here. Aware of the
presence of saintly being, drinking from a cup of clarity and holiness in a way that it is timeless.

The Christ I see in many beings and Christ I have found.
Always there have been words and symbols trying to
preserve for us the importance of fervor in the spiritual
quest. We use words like the fire of God, the Holy Spirit,
the spark of God and the Divine Fire to express the feeling.
Always it has been recognized that one must have this
kind of fervor on any holy path. It is needed for one to pur-
sue, persist and endure. Among the Hindus the word is
Agni, meaning the flame. My journey on the Agni path
has been strengthened by participating in devotion with
others so different from myself and yet so much the same.
The flame of love, devotion and intensity purifies and
guides each of us to an ever new awareness of the Inner
Presence. To me it is called Christ, to another, a different
name, but it is awakened and encouraged by all beings who
demonstrate high principles, love, clarity, compassion and
great spiritual power.
For centuries, those persons longing for closeness to
God have prayed, lit candles, fasted, chanted and stimulated the flow of adoration. Many people in our society find

it strange and awkward when the fervor of the soul breaks through the materialistic values of our day.* Yet, in the last twenty to thirty years an especially large number have felt the stirring of the heart as it reaches for something more. Many westerners, who would be shocked at Hindu chants, finger the rosary beads and chant the prayers of the West.

The many paths become one at a point of God Realization. And God Realization shows us that in God we are all one. We fan the fire of the Divine Within that we might be born again to a new level of spiritual awareness. We stand new and pure, strengthened and ready to go forward with that which is ours to do. We are now fortified with spiritual insight for the challenges of our time, both individually and as a part of the human family. Shiva, in the Hindu tradition, is the God of Fire, the destroyer of all that is impure so that the pure and real may be revealed. One must be ready to give up one's glamors and illusions, one's games and manipulations to become a clear mirror, tested and tried, which can reflect the multiple qualities of God on a daily basis. This fervent one watches for the clouds of distortion in himself and seeks to view all life with clarity.

Often believed beyond human reach, a goal unreal in itself, the path exists. The door is hidden in the crevices of life itself and only found when the heart can bleed no more and the mind ceases to judge. Now one slips to another range of expression and new realizations come. A new birth does occur. Out of sight, often unrealized for a time, the goal sought through fervor has been achieved in the inner recesses of one's being. When this occurs, there is a peace and personality glamors can fall away. The clarity of inner peace steadies the aspirant who has contacted the goal whether it can be defined or not. The spiritual energy hitting the earth at the present time is intensified, both to

---

*Today we have heard of many upper income families leaving behind fame, position and benefits, going to a small town to recapture healthy family relationships and/or values. Friends and family are shocked when such rejection of secular values is demonstrated.

awaken humanity and to prepare humanity for the challenges coming. This bombardment of holy frequencies results in "seeking" even when one does not know for what one hungers.

Today many people examine the religious rites of other faiths, seeking to find something new and different from what they have heard. An insatiable desire for something meaningful expresses itself first in mundane and everyday goals, then in the pursuit of endless relationships. Painful disappointment greets these seekers until they realize they look for the "holy of holies" within themselves. In first one, then another, the light of personal guidance begins to awaken, bringing to life a vision of the new humanity.

Call it superior intelligence, divine mind, or the plan of God, the challenges of our time require each of us to participate. The dynamic changes ahead are good, necessary and valuable and we understand them not at all. Just as the storm plays a part in the refreshing of nature, the storms of today are preparing for the new way.

The Walk-ins are messengers trying to deliver hope and help. They come in to stimulate human potential. Jesus said, "Ye are Gods,"[12] and "Even greater things than these shall you do."[13] Walk-ins are to provide a boost to humanity. These are souls awakened through human lives to awareness coming in to relieve other players because the game needs help! This is humanity's help to find creative soulutions to the critical situations humanity has created. The awakening experience causes the discovery of that inner presence which will move each into the most useful place.

A combination of false beliefs, untruths, inertia and laziness has created a consciousness so mesmerized by the material that humanity has no stimulation to "get on with it." The spiritually stimulated individuals, both so-called Walk-ins and those awakened through other means, are

---

[12]In John 10:34, Jesus quotes from Psalm 86:6.
[13]John 14:12.

right now struggling with this and being agitated to take action. Whether there are logical reasons upon which to base their feelings or not, they are all feeling time running out. The critical sense of timing and the need for action impels awakened ones to search, experiment and move about. There is that restlessness now stirring in the human kingdom that we often see as winter approaches in the animal kingdom. Whether we understand what is happening or not, we can sense "something" in the the atmosphere.

June 12, 1978

FROM THE PLANE . . .

Mountains look like handwriting in the sand.
I see the character lines in God's face.
Tears streaming down my face.
Does my God cry tears we call rivers that we drink
to live?
Perhaps so, I cry my tears to live better because
I care so.
Does the God I adore and seek, cry to give us rain
and water because that Love must flow for us to
survive?
O God, I care. I see the mountains, the wrinkles
in your brow.
The smooth plains rolling gently with your laugh.
Thank you for my life.

Section IV

The Mission

Chapter 15

"The Lord Said, 'Go'"

And the Lord said, "Go."
And I said, "Who me?"
And He said, "Yes, you."
And I said
    "But I'm not ready yet
    and there is company coming
    and I can't leave the kids
    and You know there's no one to take my place."
And He said, "You're stalling."

Again the Lord said, "Go."
And I said, "But I don't want to."
And He said, "I didn't ask if you wanted to."
And I said
    "Listen, I'm not the kind of person to get
    involved in controversy.
    Besides, my family won't like it—
    and what will my neighbors think?"
And He said, "Baloney."

And yet a third time the Lord said, "Go."
And I said, "Do I have to?"
And He said, "Do you love me?"
And I said,
    "Look, I'm scared.
    People are going to hate me
    and cut me up in little pieces.
    I can't take it all by myself."
And He said, "Where do you think I'll be?"

And the Lord said, "Go."
And I sighed,
    "Here I am, send me."

                —Author Unknown

Now that I remember more that was said to me as I stood in the presence of the Light Being what am I going to do? My personal life, so happy and good, seems to hang on a thread. Charles won't want to give up all we have and go off on a new mission. He'll never understand why I feel that I have go elsewhere and begin a new community of a different sort. Perhaps India has gotten to me. The knowingness that began as Babaji touched me continues. Every few days a new insight sufaces.

Mother Earth is in danger! Humanity is to be tested. I am to speak out! I am to create a place of greater safety and encourage others to do so also. I fight back the panic that threatens me. I don't want to begin again; life is hard enough. I am serving. I work hard; I teach; I share. I don't want to think about the future.

I find hope in waiting for Torkom Saraydarian to come to visit. He'll be here in February. We'll talk about it then. He'll tell me what to do. He knows how nicely the Villa is growing, how well I am doing, what I am accomplishing.

Charles and I have already created a spiritual community and we all are trying to practice ethical living, work on ourselves, and work in the outer world. The Villa Serena is a ten-apartment complex peopled with persons in the studies who join together each morning for meditation and almost every evening for study. We each do some volunteer work in the greater community around us, seeking to serve in the world while maintaining an attitude of love and joy. The program has grown well, over a hundred students are involved in our local area and many others travel long distances to be with us. We have students developing study groups in other cities and we make every effort to encourage and aid them. We train ministers and teachers and are gaining recognition for how knowledgeable our students are. I enjoy serving as a teacher in this way.

Why change all of this? My logical mind argues, fights and torments me. Already I know I have to move, to leave all that pleases me so. I have to take the next step.

I remember the warning I carry within the secret part of

myself. Standing in the Presence, those waves of information that permeated my being are surfacing. I feel the urgency to speak, yet I desire to be silent.

I remember Master Morya's visit and his words predicting that I'd carry a harsh message. I've already been considered strict and harsh by some. I have just reached the stability I've sought all these years. My home life is gloriously happy . . . stable. I love my husband, Charles, very much. Why do I have to get involved in controversy? I have seen myself as a mediator trying to bridge that painful place between New Age (esoteric) concepts and the more mainstream Christian approach.

I remember one morning (my notes say Sept. 1979) in meditation I was told, "In five years you'll not want to be in Flroida." I couldn't believe this. I love Florida; there is nowhere else for me. I was a child here. Florida is my home. Why would I want to leave? There's something wrong here.

By 1981 the Cuban crisis has complicated matters. Crime is soaring and racial tensions are moutning. Miami has had its first racial riots in May, 1979, and throughout the state unpleasant incidents are on the rise. This is not the Florida of the past, easy going, safe and relaxed. This is a state troubled with rapid population shifts, one of the fastest growing in the nation where city services are not keeping up with demands. Florida is changing.

Torkom arrives at the airport with a warm greeting. He's scheduled to lecture within an hour so I decide to hold any questions or comments until later in the evening. Within minutes of getting seated in the car, Torkom opens the subject. "You know you have to move, Carol, out of Florida." Again I hear myself saying, "Yes, I know." I look imploringly at him. "Please talk to me about this while you're here. I don't want to move. What do you think is going to happen?" We close the conversation.

Later that evening we speculated well into the night. The talks continue all week. The predicted times of challenge are close at hand. New Age teachers must be the first to demonstrate principles of flexibility, ecological con-

cerns, simplicity and community. Torkom stands firm in
his idea that my guidance to get out of Florida has been
correct. He is in the same predicament. He will be leaving
Agoura, California (north of the Los Angeles area) as soon
as possible. ". . . at least by the end of '82," he says. He has
chosen Sedona, Arizona. Perhaps we'd like to join him
there.

The weeks after Torkom's visit were painful and confusing. I prayed for guidance. Charles and I talked and
struggled. He was at the zenith of his career. The reno-
vation of the Villa was just recently completed. Financially
we were secure. Why not wait a few years until his retirement? Calm down, Carol. Why such a sense of urgency?

At the annual Intensive (a special week long study
period-retreat held annually for students of the seminary
program and other serious students ready for such dedicated work) in April, 1981, the subject of a major move
was disclosed. Reason for such guidance was discussed. I
shared that I was seeking guidance as to where I was to go.
A loving group from South Dakota made up of respected
students encouraged me to consider South Dakota, their
state.

A week later I had a clear guidance dream. I was in an
airport and about to go through security check. There were
three gates from which to choose. The first to the left, wide
and attractive, was labeled "Sedona." The far right, again
wide and attractive, was labeled "Rapid City," the middle
was small and plain. The sign over it said, "Other." With a
feeling of resolve I lowered my head and went through the
middle check area. I awakened knowing it would be neither
of the places I was considering.

Soon thereafter the guidance came. In my vision I was
in a large room with maps on all four sides. In front of me a
map of the U.S. filled the entire wall. My inner teacher
stands behind me and reaches over my right shoulder, his
finger directly on a spot on the map. It seems I am standing too far back to see where he points. I step up closer. I
am stunned as I see the state of Oklahoma with the name

printed clearly across the state. His finger is in the north-eastern corner of the state. My heart seems to stop. I cry out, "Oh, no, not Oklahoma . . . not OKLAHOMA!" I snap out of the vision. My heart aches. I can't believe it. I've never been in Oklahoma in my entire life.

Oklahoma is flat, dry and brown. I love the water and greenery. How can I manage? Why Oklahoma?

With a heavy heart I hesitate to tell Charles. I keep my guidance to myself for several days. I wait until a Sunday evening after dinner to tell him what I had received.

We're scheduled to fly to Sedona and visit Torkom next week. If Charles and I talk about it now we can see what he says when we go. I tell Charles and he is as stunned as I, except he shares a peculiar experience with me.

As a young man, when serving as an Air Force pilot, about age 28, a commanding officer was retiring to Colorado. Suddenly Charles had a premonition. He said to those present, "When I retire I will retire to live on a mountaintop out west." For a young man who grew up in Florida it was an unusual remark. Over the years nothing had prompted Charles to leave Florida. His family all lives in the Tampa Bay area, close together. His career advanced locally and he loves the water and sailing, flying and soaring. Florida has been perfect. Neither of us can handle much cold weather and have been raised to enjoy "southern hospitality." What would we do in another part of the country? I hear the inner voice say, "Learn."

Charles and I both were on edge as we fly to Sedona. Our moods aren't helped much as we talk of the danger of nuclear war and painful predictions. We are reading *Life After Doomsday*[14] by Bruce Clayton, an excellent book that totally supports the idea of persons surviving such an attack and makes the point that whatever happens it will be much better to be knowledgeable than to be ignorant. The book emphasizes preparedness for any emergency. It provides information on tornadoes and earthquakes. Other

---

[14]*Life After Doomsday* (New York: The Dial Press, 1980).

advice includes what to do in case of riots. How to be prepared in case of energy shortages or truck strikes that
might create food shortages or other supplies, etc. The
whole book is excellent, especially if you have avoided
thinking about these painful subjects. Arriving in Phoenix
we look foward to talking to Torkom. Will he still think the
time has come?

I share every detail of my guidance with Torkom. Patiently he listens. Charles and I wait for his response. He
smiles kindly and says, "Well, Carol, it seems you have
gotten your guidance. I think you should move to Oklahoma." I knew it was so. My last escape has been closed.
I've known all along. We try to enjoy a happy time with
friends in Arizona, but our hearts are heavy. Flying home
we agree to a plan to go to Oklahoma and see.

The community struggles with the emotions that surface. I had enjoyed living in St. Petersburg until the time
came when I began to be shown a building in my meditations. I discussed this several times with Charles. One
night, while we were having dinner, the subject came up
and he commented, "I bet I know where this building is."
We finished dinner, rushed to the location, and there it
was! It was the exact building, needing repair, but with
beautiful Mediterranean lines. We find the building is not
for sale but pursuing our interest, we make an offer. The
several out-of-state owners come to an agreement and soon
we are the proud owners of the Villa Serena. Today I happily remember the students helping in so many ways to
create a place of healing, joy and love.

We do love the building; the program is developing well;
classes are well attended and we are happy. Our dream has
come true. We suffer to think we must leave it behind. Yet,
I remember the grief of leaving St. Petersburg and how,
when I came to Sarasota, I had remarked, "I'm here until
I'm told to do something else." That time HAS come.

Everyone wants to know why I'm leaving Florida. I
have no ready answer. My guidance has been "to go." I
don't feel that it has so much to do with what's wrong with

Florida as it has to do with what I am supposed to be doing. I feel strongly that I just can't say to the public and teach to students to "Follow your inner guidance," and then, when my inner guidance says something unpleasant like this, tell it to "Sit down and be quiet, I'm comfortable here." I have to follow the inner voice or I can't maintain my own integrity. Under those circumstances if I stayed in Sarasota I couldn't teach.

Remembering . . . I know what has to be done. The time has come for spiritually awakened ones to change our society. It's no single person's task. It's our task. Everywhere the *Aquarian Conspiracy*[15] is at work. *Megatrends*[16] notes the changes as they are taking effect. It's not as it will be, but it's started. New intentional communities are social experiments of cooperation. A test to see if we can practice what we preach. All of us, who in our eagerness passionately say to God, "Give me a great mission. I'm ready," will get our chance to see how well we'll do. We always feel we're ready. We ask for the test. We feel so sure. Now the cosmic clock calls each of us into action. We shift into preparation for the change that will come.

About Thanksgiving 1980 I got some guidance after a weekend when there had been serious earthquakes in Iran. I have painted it all in full on page 224, but I particularly remember the line, "As one gives in to fear he has returned to darkness." Again and again I've been warned about the danger of fear and on the accepting of people into the community that come to "escape" something they fear elsewhere. That is not a reason to join a community. One comes to a community to live in harmony with a particular concept or lifestyle. We are seeking to create a cooperative and supportive setting where, as I have been told, we are to develop a community where we can live good lives in either the best or worst of situations.

---

[15]*Aquarian Conspiracy*, Marilyn Ferguson (California: J. P. Tarcher, Inc., 1980).

[16]*Megatrends*, John Naisbitt (New York: Warner Books, 1982).

In my mind Oklahoma was an outpost of civilization. It certainly held no attraction for me, but I knew this was mine to do. I had to go, but I did what I did from a sense of obedience. Obedience is not my long suit, but I was saying, "Okay, if this is what was shown to me I've got to go and check it out." Some of us make peace with fate easier than others. I believe I have had excellent guidance. Time and time again it's clicked in. It's worked. I've seen it, and I think some of the people that have lived around me have seen it too.

They have seen me struggle as well. My guidance comes when I get to a certain point in agony. I've described it almost like labor pains. I have to get into a certain intensity, have to have a certain amount of pain, if I can call it that, and then, all of a sudden, it's like something opens up and a plan, or a knowing, comes through. My whole spiritual growth has been caught up with the desire to know and to do. I experience a trauma that seems to work itself up into something meaningful. Then the plan becomes clear. I wish there were an easier way, but there hasn't been for me. I have to let the process come about. After knowingness comes, or said another way, once I know what is mine to do, I allow my mind to start analyzing. Usually I find the intuitive answer is always better than my logical mind could conceive for whatever reasons. My answers do not always come in the same way. Sometimes I "hear" an inner voice, or "see" a "picture." Quite often I just KNOW. This is increasingly clear for me. Sometimes I bring data back from the dream state. Always there is a feeling of inspiration or guidance that permeates the answer. Certainly with Oklahoma we have found many, many things that make sense, many things that have been logical.

Many hidden signs or subtle signs have begun to happen for us, to help us. But, it's not just this experience, I'm also basing these remarks on the guidance I have been getting over the last twenty odd years. Also, I try to be flexible enough, as a plan comes together, to allow it to adjust and live and grow and change. Lots of little pieces will come together and add to the goodness of the plan if we will avoid logically locking them out by too much rigidity.

The weekend came when Charles and I flew to Oklahoma City. We rented a car and began driving toward Tulsa. We had examined our map and were heading toward "the directed point."

As we leave Oklahoma City we are both feigning cheerfulness. We are dedicated to the test at hand and are prepared to keep a stiff upper lip. As we neared Tulsa the land was beginning to roll, green and lush. It was May and very pleasant. We had picked up a map proclaiming "Green Country" and we say, "Yes, the land is different in this area." We like Tulsa. My sense of what a city feels like responds fairly well. We begin to drive to Muskogee on the interstate. All interstates seem the same, but the land is gently rolling, green and picturesque. I remember thinking that with a few white rail fences this could be Virginia. In my guidance I had a feeling about Tahlequah. When I called home to check with my office, Susan Hyder from Atlanta had called the night before. Also, there was a message for me from Stan and Helen Ainsworth, Clearwater, Florida; both had guidance to indicate Tahlequah and the office was to let me know. All things look go . . . so it's off to Tahlequah.

Tahlequah it was. We knew when we came into town. It felt right. We got materials from a very helpful Chamber of Commerce. We found Northeastern State University. The town was small, 10,000 population. I've never lived in such a small town. The countryside is fabulous. We drove through town, turned around and drove through on another route; we checked the outlying areas. We discover rivers, creeks, mountains and woods. We find out we are in the recreational center for the state. Nestled in the foothills of the Ozarks, Tahlequah enjoys a rich Indian heritage as the capital of the Cherokee Indian Nation. In North Carolina we had heard of the Trail of Tears and the displacement of the Cherokee Indians. Guess what? This is where they came. I have great empathy. I, too, have my

trail of tears. Tahlequah was the first incorporated township in the territory. It has the second female seminary in
the country. In the mid-1800's Tahlequah was known as
the "Athens of the West." Now it is a pleasant small city
where the south and west touch. I am intimidated by the
harshness of the west, but find Tahlequah much more gentle than Arizona. The slight southern influence pleased me.
I suddenly am very aware of just how southern I am.

Originally Charles and I thought in terms of a lot of
land. To two Florida people a lot is 100 acres. Later Charles
will be the one who finds the exact piece of land. Although
we went home knowing Tahlequah was the area, Charles
subsequently flew back for a few days. He looked at properties and discussed the matter with a realtor. When the
gentleman had a couple of properties to show Charles he
came out again. Charles saw what he had and said, "No,
that's not it." They began to ride around as Charles
showed him on the map the area he wanted to explore.
Charles' own intuitive guidance and hunches, if you want
to call it that, led him to a piece of property that wasn't
listed. They went in, talked to the rancher and the rancher
showed the two of them around. As they saw the property
Charles knew this was it! He called me to fly out the next
day. When I saw Charles his face was shining; his aura
dancing. I said, "You found it." The next morning we
rented a small plane so that we could survey the adjoining
countryside. I knew it was right. Before the day was over
we had a contract on 330 acres at Sparrow Hawk Mountain. So it wasn't logic, but it was working in tune with the
plan for us. Being led by the Spirit can be a wonderful
thing just as it can be painful when you try to resist!

Since we were going to go into a new place we wanted to
have more space than we had in Sarasota. Enough land on
which to build and construct a community geared to new
ideas, as well as a place to train teachers and ministers. We
felt it necessary to think about self-sufficiency as I do
believe there will be food concerns in the years ahead. I
believe we waste space in our present day style of land use

and I know that there are some newer ideas we could find helpful. I think the cluster concept is the way of the future. It is a wise way where people can put their houses together, preserving the land, instead of every piece of land being divided up into little squares with a house in the middle. We can then provide more natural areas for wild life, birds and animals. We will have a natural setting to enjoy and we will preserve areas for farming. New land planning concepts are not an easy change to introduce. Our American sense of status makes us want more than our share. We think in a status mode. It is a very emotional issue even when we are trying to be logical.

Our community is trying to bridge that sacred place of both enjoying individual homes and sharing property. Each family will own their own homesite. A person can choose either a cluster home with little outside footage and a common courtyard or a three-fourth acre piece of land. Families with children will probably select the larger pieces. At Sparrow Hawk Village we have specifically planned to have one-third of the land reserved for farming, one-third to be used for homes, and one-third to be left in its natural state. All the riverfront property is to be left in its natural state. This means we all have an interest in protecting the riverfront. Through joint stewardship we all care what happens to the wild life, the woods and meditation cave. In this community we seek to learn to share with one another and yet each has the responsibility of supporting and maintaining their own family and life style. We are encouraging freedom and uniqueness, because we truly do believe that freeing the spark of God to express within us is what life is all about. We are choosing to come together to support each other while we grow together. We believe that all humanity is becoming one family.*

---

*See Tenet's Page.

Chapter 16

The Creation Of
Sparrow Hawk Village

Democracy is self-government.
Universal acceptance creates peace.
Understanding one another we each evolve.
Communication and cooperation create community.
Science is to serve life.
Humanity in love with life serves its creator.
Beauty begets ethical living; ethical living begets beauty.

—Guidelines for the Community
Received August 22, 1982

As the new property was being explored, the guidance came, "Pay attention to the leys* and to the energy patterns of the earth." As I had no previous experience with energy leys I was intrigued. I got maps of the property and sent them to two special friends, Terry Ross and Sig Lonegren. Both are experts in the field of dowsing, who have earned acclaim for their demonstrations of skill in this country and abroad. Each man is accustomed to working with archeologists and researchers in the use of dowsing as a technique for harnessing and gaining better understanding of the constructive earth energies. Both are aware of the ways to utilize divine proportions, the golden triangle

---

*Ley: An English term designating a sighted track of energy that can be located and traced by dowsing.

The theory is based on the ideas of streams of energy running through the earth and its etheric counterpart, similar to the concept of meridians within the body. Ley, in fact, means energy line. Ley line is redundant, although that is the expression most commonly used.

another mathematical keys to enhance beauty and proportion for the well-being of persons. Since we are interested in planning the community to live in harmony and beauty and peace, we are very pleased with the assistance they give to us.

Both feel we have a strong energy center on the property. I use this term, but in native American terminology this kind of energy center is called a medicine wheel. Such a center is made up of the convergence of a number of leys at one point. But I am getting ahead of my story.

Timing and further guidance led us to invite Sig Lonegren from Greensboro, Vermont, to come out and work with us in the location of the center. We wanted to make the most of the spiritual energies present to be a blessing to those who would come to live, visit and worship with us. From ancient times history reveals man has established places of worship on these certain lines to enhance his relationship with God and nature.

A few weeks before Sig arrived I went up on the mountain with a small set of dowsing rods. I played with them for a while but wasn't apt. I found I was more comfortable just using my hands holding them extended and walking the direction the energy led me through "feeling" it with my hands. I have realized my hands have become sensitive in this way through my work with healing. I allowed the energy to lead me. I found myself feeling as if I were standing in a fountain of water. Excited by my find I piled a stack of stones upon the place. It turned out a few days later I got a real test. In the forty-odd heavily timbered flat acres located on top of the mountain, I couldn't see through the woods to locate the spot. I started over and a second time located the highly charged area. This time I took a red bandana from one of the young people and tied it on a stick to make a flag.

When Sig arrived later he located the area in a much more sophisticated manner. It's impressive to watch him work. He looked like a young Santa with his pack on his back. He really got my attention when I saw the surveyors tools, compasses and equipment. He has several different kinds of dowsing tools and he checks, measures and maps as he goes along. The net result was that his mark was about one foot from my stones and Sig and I both expressed repsect for each other's "tools." Sometime late when Mic McKay, church architect and dowser from Rapid City, came down to study the church site, he dowsed the spot and again it had shifted back one foot toward the point I had previously located by hand.

A quick telephone call to Sig explained what was happening. Energy leys are live streams of energy that undulate slightly. The stream of a strong ley is perhaps up to two to three feet across running like an invisible river with a similar rise and fall pattern. Thus it can move its center a small bit one way or the other from day to day. As I now understand, the larger the stream, the more likely it is that this will happen.

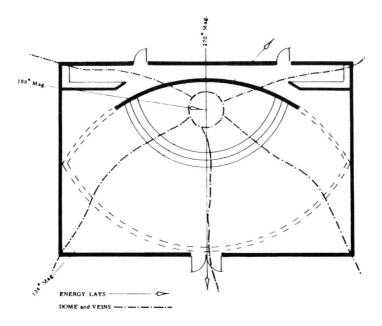

Diagram of the energy center located by Sig Lonegren and how we are utilizing it in the sanctuary.

Special attention has been given to this natural resource we found on the property and we've made every effort to appreciate God's goodness. You will appreciate the exacting details of Sig's work as you read his comments in addenda #2 of this book. For centuries spiritual centers have used precise formulas and dimensions to create sacred space and enhance the energy available to humanity. Sig helped us design the sanctuary with this in mind.

In the diagram on page 137 you can see the dome of energy located at the center of the altar. The energy leys intercept there. The veins of water are shown flowing from the dome. If you note the pattern the leys and veins make around the dome, you will see most descriptively the native American medicine wheel. The title seems appropriate for a sacred enclosure to help individuals heal and make whole their lives.

We have greatly appreciated Sig's vast store of knowledge in helping us utilize the holy ground upon which we build. Light of Christ Community Church had found its new home.

The Sparrow Hawk itself is the kestrel, the sacred symbol of the ancient Egyptians. The small hawk was chosen because it can hover and fly straight up. Thus it became symbolic of levitation and ascension.

Our graphic symbol of the Sparrow Hawk shown here was taken from a 3,000 year old wooden label found at Abydos, Egypt.

The church and fellowship hall are located on the wooded mountain top. Asthetically, the architect chose a conventional approach to construction that we can easily tie to the natural setting and that will be in keeping with the design of the cluster homes nearby. It is a good plan.

Charles asked the general contractors bidding on the church to give him an alternative bid using Solarcrete* for the walls. Charles had just discovered Solarcrete a week earlier when Jim Moore, from Minneapolis, mentioned it in a phone conversation. He checked the patient system out and discussed it with a local structural engineer. It is a new and innovative approach to wall construction and excited him immediately.

Charles was pleased when the contractor offered to try the new system at no increase in price, and promptly awarded the contract choosing this alternate. The construction workers had no experience with this new system and initially were somewhat reserved. However, they were quickly won over and some were soon planning to build themselves a new home using the concept. Charles also introduced several other "state of the art" construction techniques that have made the building a little more interesting than it would have been otherwise. The floor plan of the building is explained in the diagram below:

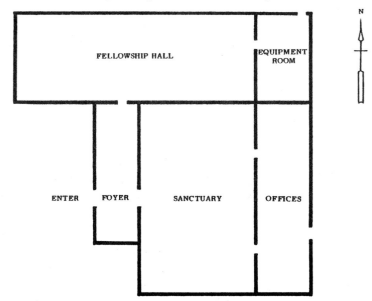

*Addenda 3 . . . Solarcrete Construction Details.

The split-level fellowship hall on the north side of the church is entered through the church foyer. It is earth-sheltered for energy efficiency and has two feet of earth over its concrete roof. In Oklahoma two feet of earth is needed to maintain sufficient moisture to grow grass. Otherwise, the soil dries out and loses its insulative value. The roof slopes up to a height of 14' against the north wall of the church, thus protecting the church from the cold north wind in winter. This 14' high wall provides a wonderful openness as well as a spectacular wall for books, art work, etc. With a library to care for and a number of artists in the group, the space is already over committed.

Church administrative offices are located on the east side of the building and are directly behind the sanctuary which faces west.

We paid careful attention to long-term maintenance as the major buildings were being planned. Realizing the complications of setting up expensive-to-maintain facilities, Charles, with his college administrative background, took special care in choosing materials and designs that would require less maintenance, especially as we expect energy and supplies to become increasingly expensive and harder to come by.

At Sparrow Hawk Village we are striving to utilize the positive aspects of technology and to develop the capability needed to survive events expected to occur during the close of the century. The possibilities of economic and social strife, increasing incidents of destructive winds, droughts and floods, severe earthquakes and volcanic activity all present a scenario that could greatly change our casual lifestyles. Predictions are numerous and though I certainly feel these concerns can be lessened greatly by the resurgence of spiritual values, our guidance has suggested we be prepared for "the best and the worst" and we are trying to do just that.

The first and foremost goal of Sparrow Hawk Village is to create an environment that fosters personal growth. The spiritual nature is best realized through the healthy integration of art, science and philosophy. We will seek to create an atmosphere of mutual sharing and support, knowing we are spiritually growing together.

Our attitude toward persons wanting to move to the village is "come and see." Talk to us and ask yourself why you would want to be here. Do you feel a pull toward the community concept or are you looking only for protection provided by others? Also, think about what you are willing to give to the whole community. How willing and ready are you to trust, follow guidance and see yourself as a steward of abundance?

I have found TRUST of major importance in community living. When we enter into closeness with others, we need to trust others and ourselves. If we have a healthy balanced sense of worth, it is far easier than it is for persons with low esteem. Great forceful egos can be irritating on others but the daily friction and loving hearts can actually handle this more easily than the low esteemed person, constantly misinterpreting each occurrence. We recognize communities need both leaders and followers and that the demands for leaders change with the occurrence of the moment. Thus we become team players!

I guess for myself I see my own role as serving as a focal point for the community. I feel obligated to be really honest, practicing tough love and calling the shots as I see them. I desire to be clear enough to know the Village isn't the right place for everyone and that we can't do everything. A major challenge I have had to learn to live with is knowing the difference between what's "mine to do" and what "is a nice thing for someone else to do." I am forced to practice discretion here and have learned to get to the heart of the matter for myself. I foresee the hard decisions of the Village down the line and know I must carry that responsibility.

The Village dare not be dependent in any one area. Likewise my guidance has been for a steering committee to be formed. These persons pray and meditate together, pursuing answers in an intuitive way for the well-being of the

community as a whole. During the spring of '82 I was given the names of those to begin such a service and they are now serving anonymously in that role. It's a position of great responsibility with no ego rewards. Each one of these works hard on self and serve in a dedicated way. The work has begun and these persons have created the highly charged magnetic oversoul needed to insure longevity and future guidance of the group.

Be aware my understanding of my present responsibility is to create the Village. I do not feel that necessarily means even if calamity struck that I would be here. It could be that I'd be in Minneapolis, New York City or London. My own guidance has been to go and do. This I am following, but as it is said many will depart the earth plane because it's not their karma to participate in coming challenges, I have had no guarantees of personal safety for myself.

I feel strongly that awakened ones are challenged to help humanity and Mother Earth. I believe that the first step is getting tuned in to God and your personal path, regardless of religious persuasion. I think a period of talking to God and listening to God is needed each day. Then I think working for God is the next ingredient. What good does it do to talk to God without listening or to listen without expressing? What kind of closeness does that create? But if the Christ Within gives us guidance then I believe we must act it out. If we are carriers of Love, Hope and Healing Compassion, we do our part by giving it away. So the active part of spiritual awakening should show in the "fruits."

At Sparrow Hawk it is not our goal to create a withdrawal community, to have a nice loving place to withdraw into from the world. A part of my whole ministry has been to interact, link up, cross boundaries, to care and to build networks. Once I was shown a map of the U.S.A. with seven prototypes of communiites being given for the coming period. I believe our pattern is one of several being developed by the Hierarchy for "the Plan." In this same way the, I think, individuals being guided to communities have to test and determine which prototype best serves them and in which type can one best serve.

Sparrow Hawk Village is ready to share its information, research, results and game plan with others who would inquire. Since I believe communities are "nice neighborhoods" and an excellent way for personal involvement, I think it is the way of the future. There are no reasons except selfishness, competitiveness, ego, status and pride that prevent any neighborhood from becoming a caring community.

After all, each church is a community of like-minded individuals, is it not? The people of each village and township should care what happens to one another. Cities are neighborhoods rubbing shoulders. I do believe now may be the time to think "small is beautiful" or at least "we are in this together." Keynotes for the New Age are cooperation, communion and community. At one time in my life when considering a major change I was told in meditation, "When you were weak, you were forced to become strong. Now you are strong. It is time to learn cooperation." I pray there are many who feel the call.

Chapter 17
The Work And The Workers

Humanity is approaching a momentous period in time. From the other (spiritual side) of life there is the clamoring of souls wanting to participate. Many, and I feel most, of the souls desirous of human life now are not beginners. These are experienced, and often highly evolved, souls who want to grow through the opportunities of the next fifty to one hundred years. These beings are ready for testing, they have knowledge to contribute; and, the inner guidance is adequately developed so that they can get back in touch as they recapitulate the body. Most of these beings are not fascinated by the materialism as we have been in the past, although many are scientific and have highly developed minds. The bright-eyed babies we are seeing are gearing up to lead the more complacent persons to peace and security through new methods.

The ascent back to God has begun. From the coming of the historical Christ and the giving of the message of Jesus to the world, a new way has been proclaimed. Few have "the eyes with which to see and the ears with which to hear." Yet, down through the darkness of the past two thousand years, the message has shone. The precious seeds of love and acceptance and wondrous words that each one is a "child of God" were planted. Group after group spoke the words but then distorted the Truth. Only a few truly believed and tried to clean their hearts and minds of prejudices and judgment. Yet the message, threatened in a thousand ways, persists. As the dawning of the New Age creeps across the heavens and into our hearts, we begin to understand those oft repeated words in a new way.

Those who proclaim they have the new way are granted a brief time in which to be heard and then the spotlight moves on. This unrelenting light points out the inconsistencies, ignorances, errors and foolishness of any prized ideology. At the same time it illumines the glittering gold of each design. We see great Truth used here and there, repetitive patterns acting themselves out. We find life lessons teaching whatever can be comprehended, then spiraling back to teach again. Each embodied soul struggles with recapitulation as it re-establishes a hold on the body, emotions and mind. It takes years to construct and reenergize these vehicles, as well as to build the base of operations for current work. As soon as a working relationship is established on the personality level, the soul can begin to have impact. For the highly aware ones this is the moment awaited. To begin again contributing the divine energies needed for human life thrills the spiritual nature. The soul pours itself into its task.

"The work," as it is called, becomes the most important reason for being. It colors alike all relationships and occupations. If one awakens to the soul presence within, the life changes and the life style and all the old values and current means of expressing have to be revamped. Each area of the life is reviewed and brought up to date.

Today the trauma of this reworking reflects itself in the spiritual pain of thousands. Combined with the restlessness of an impending sense of something special coming, we can understand the opportunity that is calling many souls to come in (Walk-in) to adult bodies to serve as focal points of inspiration.

Most of these beings who have been arriving could correctly be called "bridge people." They are those being, those aware ones, experienced in human life, who have successfully found keys to master the lower nature (physical, emotional and mental), and who have already discovered that the past prepares for the future, but must not dominate it. These people have the tools within themselves to share.

They have been given a vision to guide them, and some work in close harmony with Great Ones still in the higher worlds. Either way, we have the hierarchy of holy ones, whether embodied or standing in the wings, guiding the thousands attuned to their directions. The planetary Christ directs all the beings, so that the message delivered two thousand years ago has another chance of being heard.

This is to say that humanity has yet another chance of being saved from darkness, ignorance and materiality. Called sin by some, the absence of light (understanding, perception and spiritual insight) is darkness; it is the lack of knowing about the Christ within or the unawareness of ourselves as gods. The absence of light is ignorance. We mislead ourselves into identifying solely with our material-physical life. We delude ourselves into believing that the Game of Life is the mastery of the material-physical plane alone. The other definition of sin which I endorse is that sin means "missing the mark." If we come here to develop divine potential but forget that and only participate as a physical being, we have in fact missed the mark, or point, of having a human body.

All spiritual guidelines or teachings are to help us gain mastery over the human nature that tends to get stuck. We can get stuck in our animal nature, in our emotional pain or pleasure, or in our intellectualism. Truly spiritual guidelines present us with challenges to keep us on the edge of our seat. If we are really observing the laws of various religions, the disciplines and practices of spiritual traditions or the intricate guidance of philosophy, we will search out the impure areas of our nature. As each impurity is irradicated, additional insights come to have meaning and we are made new.

I love to point out how subtly this is at work in our lives. At one point we may smugly read the commandment, "Thou shalt not kill." Most of us really do not expect to ever violate this law, so it doesn't really speak to us. If we continue to awaken to our Christ within, we begin to realize this can mean, "Do not destroy, hurt or inflict pain on another." Still later it may mean, "Do not kill the dreams, happiness, or joy of another." For me it now means, "Do not kill the emerging being coming to life." We know we can permanently damage children by being critical of them all the time. By criticism, condemnation and negative response we can destroy the incentive, the self worth and the spirit of another.

If we can see the great meaning behind each spiritual truth, teaching or law we begin to realize the wisdom left for us by the wayshowers of humanity. And, I point out once more, we realize this is only possible for those who have the eyes with which to see.

Our school system has realized the need to have a lower student/teacher ratio for persons with learning disabilities. The higher world has decided the same thing. Since humanity has proven itself a slow learner, the ratio of awakened ones to non-awakened is being adjusted to get humanity on the move again.

Also, I believe we have to realize that the descent into matter requires far less effort than the ascent from it. Symbolically speaking, going downhill, we have the pull of gravity; being spun off into orbit, we had the thrust to whirl us outward. Now we seek to reverse that direction! It always takes more effort to change direction than to go with the momentum. Especially as the human momentum is so slow, it is easier to be engrossed in materialism than to trust our other levels of being. Our own self-doubt cancels our hopes and dreams. Our logic cancels our intuitive promptings. For some it is a challenge to believe we are a body with a spirit; the enlightened ones know we are a spirit with a body!

Only as we are enclosed in our ego centeredness can we feel superior or separate. It is being spelled out for us in daily worldwide news that we either care for the spaceship Mother Earth or she sinks, and almost all will go with her. Terra Firma, Terra Firma, we are learning! We are awakening one by one to the message.

This awakening is taking place in every aspect of human

living. Whether it be in education, philosophy, religion, art or science there is a restlessness with which to be dealt. This unsettledness, this call to the perimeter of understanding will stretch us to the point of a painful breakthrough in every facet of societal life.

The building of the future is humanity's work. If this group consciousness can learn what co-worker really means, all the other energies, entitites, and evolutions can join in, but humanity is challenged to respond to its reason for being.

Others can encourage, support and inspire. But the test humanity is being called to take will be taken and humanity will reap its result. That is the law of divine order.

The 60's and 70's frightened scores of people as many Americans rebelled, stretched, broke through the entrenched borders of authority. Not because authority or perimeters were bad, but because the rigidity demanded resistance. Now we have to rethink, redefine, reevaluate the worth of all human values. It is easier for the slightly awakened to go back to sleep and let it all go by, but enough of us have been jarred badly enough to keep asking the questions. Most of humanity would like to go back to sleep, but those men and women who set change into motion called for help. It was really humanity's cry for help. The call is being answered. The Walk-ins, the angels, the hierarchy, the forces of Light are here now as invited guests involved in providing assistance to Terra and humanity.

Chapter 18

Awaken To The Plea

My experience of waking up as a Walk-in has been very similar to "time capsules" going off. A bit of information would be revealed and I would experience a recall of another time, remembrance of previous knowledge which would result in a leap of expanded consciousness.

I would adjust my viewpoint of life to include the new data. For awhile my perspectives would stabilize with the incoming data, then another piece of the puzzle of my emerging life would fall into place for me.

The decision to share some of this information in a book has been a formidable one. Who would dare, or care, to reveal that there is an "inner voice" to which you listen? What purpose would it serve? This inner secret seems so incredibly precious and private that the biblical words apply: "Do not cast your pearls before swine." And yet, for me, my PROMISE to the Light Being was to do just this . . . but only if there was a true need for others to hear. Therefore the decision was made because I realize how incredibly important the story is for these two audiences.

First, I would share with other Walk-ins who are trying to arrive at an understanding of their own experience and mission. These souls are intense personalities feeling increasing pressure to do something. Frequently the intellect hasn't consciously received the message about the mission. I would like to bring relief to these Walk-ins. I am hopeful some will be able to identify with my story and feel a similarity and a recognition. If these messengers can awaken to themselves and gain understanding, they can get on with their mission.

The Walk-in must get over being dazed and disoriented by the shifts within himself; then he can begin to be of value. Each individual struggles to bring in his/her remembrances of what is "known" from elsewhere. A major problem the Walk-in has to deal with is in not having someone "outside" to confirm these rememberings. When those persons around the Walk-in deny the possibility for different realities, consciously or unconsciously, the Walk-in deals with personal feelings of "differences" or "non-acceptance." The experiences continue and the newly arrived one has to either get strong and accept the personal reality being built, or surrender to great depression and confusion.

There is a second group I hope will listen. This group is comprised of the spiritually stirred people from all walks of life from around the world who feel or sense a crisis in the making. In the U.S. and elsewhere a number of respected human potential educator and spiritual teachers have acknowledged their concern about either nuclear war, economic break up, civil unrest and/or earthquakes and other natural events leading to undoubtedly painful human experiences. These spiritually stirred people, everyday persons as well as politicians, diplomats, artists, educators, journalists, visionaries, mystics, spiritual teachers and some scientists, feel compelled to point out at least two paths to the human future. If we have an option, and I believe in some areas we do, should not these persons be heard? Certainly we should want to hear dangers defined and *solutions aired.*

My belief is that humanity is standing, now poised, trying to make the decision either to fight it out in a great and destructive finale for our modern civilization or to decide that peace can be greater than war. Can government leaders work toward cooperation, common concern, health and peace-keeping policies? Or will each country stockpile weapons because of its fear of vulnerability? Can any country allow itself to support peaceful measures rather than threaten to push the "hot button?" These spiritual attitudes are as confusing for the man in the street today as were many other worldwide causes in the past, such as equality, opposition to slavery and voluntary water rationing. Suspicion, distrust and thoughts of superiority dominate the American way of life. We are rapidly approaching a time when whole societies must awaken.

My guidance has been that the attitude humanity forms between February 1982 and January 1984 shapes the challenges we face during the rest of this century. I think any spiritual work we do on ourselves or in society at this moment registers in humanity's "book of life." Prayer, meditations, acts of service, ethics are all important. Jesus specifically said, "Love one another," and the acceptance of this ideal can heal a great many injustices. New Age teaching sugests that in the age ahead we'll live in peace and cooperation. This may mean we will have a disastrous war and those left will clean up and will learn to co-work. It may be that nature will become so vicious in its cleansing, humanity will learn to co-work to survive. As I am writing this book (December '82), the television is showing pictures of Denver digging out of its Christmas day blizzard; Minneapolis slowed to a crawl by an early severe winter blizzard; and Louisiana and surrounding areas ravished by flooding. In each news broadcast pictures show concerned workers helping others and teaming up to save property and lives. The threat of nature unites. Disaster awakens us to other values.

The simple acts of prayers for peace, full moon meditations, visualizations and affirmations have great power. I think it becomes increasingly important that we seek the higher, wiser WILL, not our own. I ask my students to daily say the Great Invocation.

From the point of Light within the Mind of God
Let Light stream forth into the minds of men
Let Light descend on Earth.

From the point of Love within the Heart of God
Let love stream forth into the hearts of men.
May Christ return to Earth.

From the center where the Will of God is known
Let purpose guide the little wills of men—
The purpose which the Masters know and serve.

From the center which we call the race of men
Let the Plan of Love and Light work out
And may it seal the door where evil dwells.

Let Light and Love and Power restore the Plan on Earth.

If you have no specific message as to what is yours to do, let's do the loving and purifying work on self and be available for the service which opportunity presents, until you can hear the inner voice. I believe we are now in a time which is to allow us to awaken, cleanse and change humanity's destructive pattern to one which will be less painful.

I still ask, however, are there enough thinkers awaking from the lethargy of materialism to realize where our present acts and attitudes can be taking us? Daily, new voices are joining the cry for peace, for ecological concerns and for careful appreciation of resources.

If enlightened ones are not able soon to have a great impact on the masses they face a second responsibility. They are to create pockets of persons committed to holding high principles during the years ahead. I personally do not believe humanity will be wiped out by a nuclear war, but I certainly believe an incredible challenge awaits the survivors.

But, I vote for survivors whether it makes sense or not. I believe, in this case, a new attitude will emerge and persons needing one another will be able to find cooperative union.

In fact, I believe the New Testament supports such thought although it is still unclear and confusing to almost everyone. Enough predictions of natural destruction exist to give us cause for alarm even without the bomb. My feeling is that if humanity follows the lead of developing cooperative groups and rejects the idea of war, working through the arguments inherent in that situation, we, by the power of our mind, will decrease many of the predicted earth traumas. This is the changing on the mental/emotional level that can lessen the breaking up or cleansing that the earth needs.

I feel the records of today's scientists support stepped-up seismic activity. I believe the records of crime's increased percentages already reflect the rising trauma in the mind of humanity; suicides, abortions, divorces, and homicides indicate the increasing trauma in the mental and emotional life.

Most sincere religious and spiritual persons feel that a return to God, to spiritual values and to moral living is the way to correct these ills. We are aware, however, that many of these persons calling themselves "God's people" condemn one another, destroy respect for universal ideas, hate other races and religions, plant seeds of suspicion on every path but their own. Without change, the same lack of love and trust will be perpetuated. In this type of leadership we see all the painful and destructive qualities of a human consciousness, sick and in despair.

Esoteric (metaphysical) philosophy has guidelines which explain how our human consciousness creates our experiences. This is as true about mundane weather storms as about personal illnesses and troublesome relationships. Those who accept these principles may have strong feelings and/or confusion as to how to face such a vision of destruction in a spiritual manner.

I believe a number of Walk-ins are specifically charged with the responsibility for creating peaceful communities for the training of the second group, the spiritually awakened persons. Their first task is to create a sufficient impact on the secular world so as to develop new values and new understanding which would lead to peace rather than chaos. They must also train people to serve as New Age leaders should humanity choose to turn away from the old age ideas of separation and materialism.

Here are three ways of saying that this is the moment for which humanity has waited:

1. The externalization is happening . . . now and every day . . . through Walk-ins and through the revelation of the high consciousness of others already in body, as the highly charged etheric substances reflect and resound with creative force.

2. Angels are walking among men and not much of humanity has the eyes to see them yet. Challenging stories, sincerely told, may not change things much, but to the few who have been made ready, it is given. Walk-ins can be the manifestation of "Spirit beings" or of angels spoken of in Hebrews 13:2. ("Remember to show hospitality. There are some who, by so doing, have entertained angels without knowing it.")

3. The incoming souls we are calling Walk-ins are members of the Disciples of the Christ . . . the long promised representatives coming to earth to prepare humanity for the *Reappearance of the Christ.*[17]

These beings or messengers are co-working with the Hierarchy, receiving the message from the higher world and stepping it down to those ready to hear. Called the Disciples of the Christ they release the Light, Love and Power of Transformation to those ready to participate in creating the "new heaven and new earth." Certain souls committed to work in this way have been entering since June, 1945, when the Christ announced he would emerge again into physical contact with humanity.

His servers seek to prepare the world for his reappearance even though they know not the day nor the hour. The preparation required of humanity before the emergence is being guided by the disciples at this time.

Out of the chaos of the old, the phoenix does arise.

---

[17]*The Reappearance of the Christ* (London and New York: Lucis Publishing Company, 1974), Chapter 3.

Chapter 19

Living With The Message
And The Messengers

Awareness is a quality resulting from an expansion of consciousness. As this occurs with the Walk-in, the expansion is so great, the new perceptions which flood the mind are so dazzling, that a struggle results to find a way to confirm the information. Walk-ins have to deal with insights which significantly change the reality that has been experienced by the outgoing soul.

The message is now going out for Walk-ins to step forward. The major reason for this is two-fold:

1. To help other Walk-ins proceed on with their duties. This can't begin without self-acceptance.

2. To reassure the public of God's plan working out on Earth. At a time of emotional trauma, which many already sense, it is easy for persons to give in to the despair, doubt and gloom so readily available.

The soul sent in to reassure humanity and to help lift this heavy veil tries to point out the existence of higher worlds, tries to actualize love and support in the immediate moment, tries to confirm God's love for all, and tries to give some immediate directions to society as "how-to's" for the changes ahead.

The Walk-in seeks to stimulate those he/she can inspire to look at situations in new ways. The ability to perceive new and innovative solutions grows in the contemplative or philosophical mind. The willingness to look takes courage and it is a choice often rejected by mass consciousness so easily intimidated by anything painful or unpleasant.

The exercise of looking at all the options helps a person expand and grow both emotionally and mentally. If we can confront a paralyzing fear it may spur us on to the first steps of action. If enough persons are so moved, then humanity is choosing to do something regarding its fate. As we think through our fears and we learn that we have options, the trauma begins to lessen. In this way some helpful ideas will be produced, and if the worst occurs, those who have processed these thoughts will not be as frightened or helpless. The unthinking public which has not even considered the consequences will be caught in the traumatized wave-length of fear.

I meet people regularly who are saying that only recently have they begun to hear on public news about the danger or possibilities of nuclear war. I would ask everyone to realize that it is only when we begin to hear something that it enters our reality. We become "aware" . . . it seems we hear the same thought everywhere. This always occurs as we expand and consciously embrace new ideas. We are prone to say, "It is an idea whose time has come," when in reality the idea has been around a long time. It is simply now "our" time to work with that information.

Undoubtedly, ever since humanity became self-conscious, it has been challenged to become at peace with death. Every culture has established its own way of dealing with this phenomenon. We have formed rituals for both the deceased and survivors. Generally, humanity has experienced death as a great enemy and is terribly confused when confronted with those wishing to embrace the experience. Probably the person eager to walk into death's outstretched arms scares us most of all.

Also, those talking of death as desirable, stir within us the deepest feelings of alienation and confusion. We haven't been able to relate to the Buddhist who sets himself on fire, or the one who fasts to death for a cause. Our innermost resistance to death is challenged! How can anyone dare to go willingly into the void?

Today many are saying life can be worse than death. Mystics claim something more exists. Religions repeat the message. Psychics, spiritualists and parapsychologists try to explain phenomena. Ideologies are shared. Personal stories are told. Scientists are studying the Near Death Experience in an attempt to get an understanding of the reality of which many now speak.

Is there a logical or spiritual reason for the recent (especially the last 150 years) surge of interest in this area? Are the Walk-ins challenging us more and more to look at the experience in a new way? Could humanity be moving forward to a time when it will need to know that the physical life is only a part of the whole life, and not even the most important part?

If the prophecies of the many sacred writings are ticking off their indicators, as many seem to think, perhaps the exercise of making peace with death is a vital part of our preparation. Any of us who happen to witness a disaster is suddenly stretched to compute the loss of persons, damage to physical surroundings, and loss of valuables and dreams. As our personal world is ruptured by the happening, we first reel from the blow, then survey the setting and next hopefully, shift into action.

Persons who have never met hardship have greater fear. Persons least prepared feel the greatest inadequacy. Those of us who have been through tough moments have had basic training. The recovered widow/widower is the one who knows and understands when another loses a mate. The parents of dead children reach out with caring support to parents in similar circumstances. I think of the people who have had colostomies or mastectomies who quietly share in order to help others carry on.

As a group, if we can expand our reality to accept death as a part of life, we free ourselves from great suffering. Our survival instinct can still exist by choosing good health habits and resisting carelessness.

Somehow, we falsely believe that if death is acceptable, it will claim more of us sooner. In fact, the opposite seems to be true. Having made peace with death, it seems we can turn to our business of living with more energy and more dedication. We move the energy that once held our mind away from the subject of death into activities of our choice. Should our attention be drawn to the question of death, we can look clearly at today's issue without trauma welling up from unopened compartments in our subconscious.[18]

If humanity's future includes earth changes, social unrest, and perhaps nuclear war, the death and dying movement will be boot camp. This may be the opportunity to "be prepared." Everything that we can work through in our lives on a daily basis now, will serve us well if our world becomes even more chaotic. We know that all we integrate helps us time and time again.

Training for the future seems to include flexibility, inner connection to guidance and a belief in life in a new way. A river twists and turns lazily through its boundaries until the storm, when suddenly, this formerly peaceful friend charges about like a maniac, unmindful of its rightful place. People living along the banks must not take its pattern for granted. We must remember the challenges of the past and have an unlimited awareness and enough information to form a plan for action.

My information is that humanity gets to vote, at least in part, on its future. The law of karma declares that certain issues must be dealt with. The teachings of grace suggest that if we can change our consciousness, we no longer require certain responses. We can alter the future by altering our conscious course. There would be no need for prophecy if everything were predestined.

The future arrives through will and fixed design. The seasons represent the fixed designs of rhythms and cycles we all expect and have come to trust. We wrestle with the will aspect as creators-in-miniature, not always understanding what we want or what it will cause in the long run.

---

[18]*A New Age Handbook on Death and Dying*, Carol W. Parrish-Harra (California: DeVorss and Company, 1982).

We vascillate, hesitate and see-saw until we cause, for our-selves, as well as others, the conflicts we experience. Life moves slowly forward balancing the effects of will and design. These laws seem not to register clearly to us until we can stand in the objective posture usually attained through philosophical thinking or spiritual stretching.

In a conversation last spring about the possibilities of Walk-ins, Dr. Kenneth Ring, noted scientific researcher in death and dying, raised a most valid point. He speculated, from a scientific viewpoint, that the shift in consciousness experienced in the NDE has the effect of "an individual seeming like a new person, when in fact they were not." This is realistic, for I do not find that all persons who ex-perience the NDE are Walk-ins. For some individuals the NDE is such an enormous breakthrough in awareness that the rest of the physical life is spent in integrating this powerful experience. I believe for many, the new ideas and feelings which occur become the first step in identifying with expansion of consciousness.

As we study the impact of the NDE upon the lives of in-dividuals we see profound changes. Often there is little memory of much more than a motion, a presence and an en-counter with a familiar messenger. The power of such an experience is so intense it doesn't matter that it cannot be put comfortably into any framework. A profound inner knowing emerges. When this re-awakens interest in life it creates a deeply stirred individual.

In some of these people the Walk-in experience has oc-curred. There are many incoming souls who are taking ad-vantage of this process. It provides an excellent oppor-tunity for quick entry in order to help humanity. I should point out that Ruth Montgomery says Walk-ins are using other mystical experiences of despair and transformation to enter, in addition to NDE. As an example, another type of entry is through the religious conversion experience when one goes through the agony of catharsis and sud-denly a great peace enters the personality. Also, it can oc-cur in moments of ecstasy or wherever powerful spiritual force separates the consciousness of the personality from the soul. Other periods of unconsciousness resulting from various causes can serve this purpose as well. These are not as easily apparent as near death experiences. Remember the key is the intense desire to die, the experience itself, and then the beginning again in a much more positive vein. I believe that this can occur whenever life is threatened if death has been desired and that the souls have received help and/or permission from the Lords of Karma to utilize this opportunity. The incoming soul must believe it can convert this life into a meaningful experience for the good of all.

As minds are opened to these new perceptions, be aware that the Near Death Experience may be seen as the death and resurrection spoken of in various ancient mystery traditions. I can easily see the reason for looking at such a critical and profound experience in this way. NDE's have certainly proven this much: it is the death of the old and the beginning of the new for many who have undergone such a phenomenon.

If the Near Death Experience serves to totally change the person, if the term and concept of a new soul in an old body is too much, try thinking that the personality named "XYZ" died and the soul level now stands revealed. This blessed one, tender and made new, has been freed from the old self to be allowed to become a new self.

I fervently hope that those scientists on the edge of new understanding will examine these individual experiences without the rejection traditionally met from the scientific fields. As more and more people share their NDE's, telling of their visions of the future and giving certain prophesies,[19] they are still being met with the old patterns of suspicion and fear. May the courage of dedicated scientific explorers continue to forge into these challenging areas to find and prove what more exists within the mystery of humanity's mind.

---

[19]May 25, 1982. Paper. "Precognitive and Visionary Aspects of Near Death Experiences," by Kenneth Ring, Ph.D., Professor of Psychology, University of Connecticut and President, ISANDS. Delivered, The Academy of Religion and Psychical Research.

Chapter 20
The Why And How Of "Walk-ins"

The Aquarian Age spells death to the former Piscean Age human consciousness. The new energies bombarding our planet today demand that we work together in a spirit of cooperation. At the critical point of entry into the time of the Piscean Age, humanity was forced to leave behind a group consciousness that was an instinctual, group lower mind awareness. It was forced to move to an individualized self-consciousness in its evolutionary pattern of growth. Now mankind must relinquish the emphasis on individual self authority and move once again to a group consciousness. This time, however, it will be a move to an awareness of the comfort and harmony inherent in this opportunity for co-working and co-creating.

I believe this pull to become one cooperating humanity is appearing everywhere around the world. This energy is encouraging us to link up, to become aware that the action of one (person, group, country) affects many others. That "no man is an island" is being shown to us again and again. Sociologically, scientifically and philosophically we are learning of our interlocking ties. We are finding the interdependencies of all humanity and all nature emphasized in countless ways due to the ignorance of our past consciousness. In recent years the ecological movement has had a dramatic emphasis as the outer, material world has pointed to this new idea pushing humanity to cooperate with itself and other forms of life on the planet.

Inwardly, we are becoming more aware of our sameness in pain and in joy. Through television we become more in-

formed about other life styles and cultures, we see human
suffering around the globe and we observe the celebrations
of life expressed through a myriad of races, religions and
personal quests. We begin to identify with all of mankind
through the powerful emotional nature we share. As we do
this, we can now dare to allow our sensitive and caring
nature to emerge. We see ourselves, our fears and our
hopes reflected wherever we look and we begin to know
Life as the great teacher.

A major message of the Aquarian Age emphasizes the
creative power we carry, urging us to become aware of ourselves as co-creators with God. We must understand in a
new way that each action has a reaction. We must create
for others as well as for ourselves. We must become team
players, linking ourselves into constructive patterns, thus
demonstrating high concern for the standards or truths we
proclaim.

This message proclaims the need to free ourselves from
hypocrisy, to truly become what we claim to be, to move
from possessing and controlling attitudes to generous giving, sharing and positive action. Much later, the move will
be to simply "being." This complete acceptance in harmony with the influence of the High Self within is positive
and supportive. The state of "being" takes less energy and
creates no stress.

New Age teachers often say the Sermon on the Mount
was Jesus' great proclamation of Law. As Moses delivered
the Ten Commandments to his people, so Buddha taught
the Noble Path and the Eight-Fold Truths. Even today, as
we study the biblical books of Matthew and Luke, reading
the Beatitudes[20] and trying to comprehend the meaning of
such guidelines, we struggle to gain the needed insight into
what often appears as merely platitudes. As we grow in
spiritual awareness, these teachings will take on more and
more meaning and will become clear.

While esoteric teachings say humanity is lagging behind

---

[20]Holy Bible: Matthew 5:3-12 and Luke 6:20-23.

in its maturing process, Walk-ins, teachers and the awakened are proclaiming the danger of such stagnation. Humanity is resisting change and enlightenment. It clings to the darkness of the material stage, not able to find its way through the maze. The human nature has built so much desire and affection for the dense material world, it has veiled itself from the Light. The two principle energies necessary on the "ascent back to God" or the "return of the prodigal son to his Father" are Love and Will. These two create perimeters within which we can live our lives in a beneficial and progressive way.

Love, which is the first and greatest commandment, can change our world and our own reaction to the world. Songs like "What the World Needs Now," "Impossible Dream," "Imagine" and many others herald this theme, yet to be a loving, caring person challenges us deeply. We think about, talk about and proclaim we are somewhere in a part of the process of becoming. The worldwide search for love reflects so clearly our struggle. We are trying to become beings of "love and caring."

Our other challenge is to develop our will and to learn to use it for the well-being of ourselves and others. No longer is the will just to empower, but now, it also becomes our rudder as we move through life. With our will we safely steer our actions according to the standards we have consciously chosen. As we learn to work together we can "will" harmony, protection and work for the well-being of individuals and for the group mind of humanity, in ways which are unthinkable today. An example of this would be the use of government funds for hospitals, water systems and food development rather than for military operations. The military would be a public service organization of great benefit if our concepts should grow and expand into the beneficial possibilities. *The choice of creative thinking* is one message to which humanity will be required to respond.

Often the fear of the future, the unknown, pushes us backward. For some, secure in the successful manner in which the intellect has served, dare not violate reason and accept a belief of life "beyond." Yet, others feel challenged to give up old symbols, favorite toys and games, old hurts and favorite indulgences. Already many are feeling this pull toward the future.

We need to recognize how much the past has meant, how important it is for all humanity to integrate its lessons so that we can move on to the next stage. Just as a child moves through infancy to adolescence, from young adult to elder, humanity evolves too. We have been stuck at the "teenage" for a time and now we are trying to mature, to awaken to a more responsible position. We certainly do not wish to destroy our future opportunities, yet so few have opened their next stage of mind to their potential. The cry, "Wake up humanity!" comes from all who know.

Physicists, psychologists and mystics find themselves again and again experiencing similar insights and knowledge through their particular disciplines. While my way is of the mystic, I rejoice at the similarity of the tune. If we can hear the melody through the various vocabularies, the message sounds familiar.

Spiritual messages suggest there are spirals which we travel. Moving in a system of cycles age after age, we repeat patterns, gradually mastering limitation, acquiring knowledge, overcoming temptations, establishing pattern after pattern, and then refining each. We see the rise and fall of nations, the conquests and the defeat of peoples.

This spiraling action, ever upward, gradually lifts us into an awareness of the Divine Plan. When history repeats itself without creative input (inspiration, prophecy, intellectual genius), we find humanity going in circles.

In our recent history we observe that humanity has been unable to improve much on its level of response to situations, although it has certainly improved its technology with which to continue in its circles.

Awakened ones seek to evoke a new response—the inflow of evolved souls or heavenly helpers comes to awaken the human awareness to the dangers of continued circles and to the potentials of new genius. BREAK FREE is the command. Dare-to-be-divine.

The New Age calls for the freedom of seeing souls as souls, not objects to move around like chess pieces. People of heart centeredness won't fight wars . . . that's an act of solar plexus, competitive centeredness. The incoming vision calls for caring what happens to others even at personal discomfort and inconvenience. It calls for getting involved, making people uncomfortable, voting, peace marches and equality.

The destructive myths of the past must be de-energized. None of them can be used now. Some of the wisdom which has served humanity on its descent into matter won't serve on the ascent.

We have to reevaluate. As we bring together our intellect and our inner mind and stand in that Light of high consciousness, we can escape the games and follies of the past. Only then can we create a new way.

It is the cleaning up that gets tough. It is easier to believe a lie heard a thousand times than the Truth told once. I've always said that after living in a house a number of years it is easier to move than to clean and redecorate.

Yet this shape-up/clean-up act is humanity's to do. You might say it is our karma to clean out the basement, the desires and the dreams. In the midst of the clean-up, we will find the inspiration of extended minds. We will discover our part, our place of service.

Call it superior intelligence, divine mind or the plan of God, the New Age requires each of us to participate. The dynamic challenges ahead are good, necessary and valuable and, as yet, we understand them not at all. Just as the storm plays a part in the refreshing of nature, our storms of today are preparing for the new way.

Those who hate change and cling to the past will bring to themselves and others hard tests and great pain before they will release their fixation on the old way and move into their own rightful pattern for their future. Fear paralyzes, thus the more fearful one becomes, the less he is

capable of making the needed change or of finding the
answers he seeks.

It is often suggested that the problem carries within
itself the solution. This suggests that we will find the needed answers existing right within the groups having the experience. Family members needing help must look to other
family members for support, encouragement and love. The
inventions you and I have so enjoyed have been created by
individuals, awakened to new ideas. If humanity has new
needs, it is the creative consciousness within humanity
that is duty-bound to discover the way to meet those challenges. The human genius is capable of every need.

The secrets or keys needed to guide humanity out of the
maze are here among us. Just as Edison had hidden within
him the secret of the light bulb, our answers are here. The
many pieces needed to meet the challenge of power struggles, political unrest, food shortages and nuclear war are
here in the minds of human beings, only waiting to be un-
earthed, evaluated and supported.

The mosaic of the "new heaven and new earth" is here.
You have a piece and so do I. We may not have found it yet;
it may need to be unwrapped and recognized. If we give up
or stop searching, our contributions will never be made. If
we get taken in by the beliefs of the past, we'll try to "let
God do it," without our help. If we can't beat our swords
into plowshares because we may need them next year for a
war, the quantum leap forward won't happen.

Perhaps it takes the threat of a nuclear disaster to help
us throw out the possibility of solving problems through
war. Perhaps it takes the horror of acid rains, smog and
polluted rivers for us to become respectful of Mother
Earth. Perhaps it takes energy shortages and high prices
for us to look at the sun for our energy. It seems all of this
is necessary for humanity to appreciate in a new way the
blessings we have taken for granted. Much of humanity
allows itself to be comforted by the idea of the second coming and the return of the Christ to get us off the hook. It
may well be it is the Christ *within us* that has to do what

must be done.

Perhaps the most difficult to understand yet the most essential aspects to realize about the Walk-ins and the pattern they have picked can be summarized with these few important thoughts. These beings begin their mission operating on the keynote of the predecessor. The builder of the body had certain karma, good and bad, and certain challenges (lessons to learn) and obligations (debts). That builder had made certain commitments to other souls prior to coming in. These would fall primarily in the area of relationships to others: as a parent, a child, a mate, a business partner, or even as a competitor, as well as supporter, benefactor, mentor, etc. This pattern has been designed by the Karmic Lords for the builder of the body to grow through these experiences. Now he/she determines they "have had it." For whatever reason they want OUT. There are always certain options open to the human soul. Slow death . . . willing it either consciously or unconsciously, suicide, deadly attitudes, destructive health practices, etc., are familiar choices. Often we even realize that we, or others, are dealing with death wishes . . . consciously or unconsciously.

Now as this is taking place, a different soul may decide it can change that life into a meaningful mission. If there is a reason beneficial to the group it may get the help of the higher ones in making an exchange. This is a major consideration and we do not really understand just how these higher decisions are made, except it is known the ultimate reason for entering is not for the pleasure, growth or well-being of the personality. This is not to say these may not occur, but the thrust of the life has to be built around a contribution to humanity and a dedication to service. Ultimately, this is the key to spotting the Walk-in. There will be a humanitarian focus that is intense and obvious.

The incoming soul has to agree to complete lessons currently implanted in the pattern set into motion by the outgoing soul, and agrees to work out some major details that exist in the design that has been already put into the ethers. This is a credit to the outgoing soul in return for its service of exchange being rendered to the higher cause of humanity. Only now, if the energies of the two souls can be synchronized, do we have the framework for an exchange.

Challenges for the incoming soul are picking up relationships and resolving them and healing, repairing or living with a physical vehicle that has to be repaired or sustained which is not entirely his/her own. Delicate physical bodies very often are a mark of the Walk-in if the other ingredients are present. The Walk-in has to "know" the vehicle and how to handle it consciously, never putting it on "rote" as the majority of people can. Facing the limitations that are built into the basic design, the incoming one lives with an inherited sex, nationality, education and cultural heritage. While some of this can be altered and upgraded, the basic format is already established.

If we remember we are always casting the long shadow for what our future will be several years ahead, we begin to see why it takes some time for the incoming soul to achieve stability and to make its own impact. The tone (keynote or vibration) that goes out through the cosmos when the composition begins (for the original soul) can *not* be re-sounded. The incoming vibration can raise, lower, lengthen, or adjust the note. Part of the karmic pattern to a life is set by the moment of birth* (the energies available or the possibilities, as we generally say). Part of the pattern is set by the karmic ties to parents; we call this the genetic heritage. These perimeters of the life also include the point in time when one enters and the struggles of the society at the time of entry. This is the fixed design with which any entering soul has to work. Now, when the exchange happens, all those perimeters remain.

The incoming soul can only *gradually* release into that framework the new and different energies of the intuitive, atmic and divine planes that it may have access to, or the possibilities exist for burn up or blow out of the gifted personality vehicle. Just as we speak of every cell in the body

---

*See Section V: Astrological-Numerological Data.

being made new in seven years, the Walk-in begins and first stabilizes his/her ability to work within the personality framework. Later it adjusts the vehicles to the new frequencies and sets about establishing the new particulars which will guide the life toward the mission. While this altering is being done, the Walk-in faces learning to deal with physical life in a rapid time frame rather than in the norm. It is challenged to pick up the current relationships and work them to the best conclusions and to fulfill obligations as well as possible within the karmic ramifications of the original life. Since the Walk-in usually is wiser, though I hasten to say it may not always be so, the relationships and challenges that were so defeating before are now faced and resolved in the face of the incoming wisdom.

By the time a cycle of seven to nine years has been completed (a point numerologists should address*), hopefully the new being (the Walk-in) has established control of the situation and is facing the events of the fixed design from a different and more aware point of view.

Now the two lives, the remnant of one and the beginning of number two, are merged. The second soul is guiding the life and making maximum use of its reasons for entering into the fixed design of the first personality. Relationships are now truly converted to the new soul. These souls have been intertwined for a cycle (seven to nine years) so they are no longer NOT relatives, but true relatives and just as closely interwoven as adopted children/parents or friends we choose lovingly. If the incoming soul cannot upgrade the relationships to the new soul frequency, relatives will assume the role of acquaintances with whom there is no special response or rapport. In seven to nine years the incoming one has either established upgraded ties with relationships or it will not. Any ties held must adjust to the present new soul frequency. For this reason the astrological data remains valid and the numerology insights can still be

---

*See Section V: Astrological-Numerological Data.

used. Just as the palm pattern of each individual's hand gradually changes, charts reflect possibilities and we see the wise soul making the most of them. As we watch we see the level of life shift from the mundane to the magnificent.

It is important to realize that each life pattern has potential built in. At the same time each human soul carries its own seeds of karma. In one life a soul rarely works out all its potential, but chooses the lessons as the seeds (of karma) develop. We recognize that, as with all souls, in some situations we completely solve (dissolve), while others we do with as much as we can and sometimes, in some cases, we make matters worse. Still, through all of these we grow and learn.

When the outgoing soul leaves certain karmic seeds partially developed in the pattern, the incoming soul has to deal with these as best it can. By the time a cycle has been completed these situations have been resolved and the seeds that came in with the newly arrived soul have germinated and begun to flourish. From outer observation Walk-ins are seen as rapidly changing; from the inner, we are rearranging the furniture of the life to serve the new occupant.

Chapter 21

Mine To Share

Writing my story has been an exercise in agony. Only when one considers the "coming out of the closet" which it requires, can one realize the anxiety it brings up from within me.

After having spent years becoming acceptable so that I could get into the posture needed to do what I came to do, (Spring 1981) the inner message comes to "lay it all on the line!"

Only the urgency of our times can cause persons such as myself to speak out so nakedly. It is hard today for our society to believe what the ancient wisdom teachings say in all great religious books. How much more difficult it will be to accept the Walk-in messenger who tells you, "I say this is so."

The crisis years now upon us demand that by our life example we vote to continue life on this planet, or extinguish it. We, as thinking and caring adults, must act to create a new social awareness or it will never be. Materialistic, selfish views can no longer dominate the earth or she'll throw us off! The earth as a living being has been tormented to the limit. We are like fleas destroying our host. It's time we care what happens to the dog!

I believe that to speak out is an effort to stop the headlong rush into crises we cannot even imagine. In hundreds of ways we are setting up violations of God's laws.

Walk-ins are coming by the thousands to cry out from every educated post of work: Stop! Care! Today, through this book, I am struggling to speak my part; tomorrow another person with different credentials, will speak the same message. The resounding cry becomes louder: hate destroys! It contaminates and kills both its creator and its victim. Fear paralyzes the flow of creative inspiration that is needed to sustain us as we would work ourselves to the new higher level of standards life in modern society is capable of producing.

It is only a fool who can believe he can exist alone in any kind of life worth living. Some arrogant individuals still believe their personal power can save them. Why, it can't even make us happy. It certainly can't enrich the inner being. Just as the seed needs water and light to sprout, the high consciousness needs to love someone for unselfish reasons to flourish. The work, the effort, the struggle to serve another person, cause or principle, begins to transform the lover. We change.

Mystics use symbols to present their insights because the symbol can preserve the message for great periods of time. The monasteries of the Middle Ages sought to preserve the finest thinking for the future through the symbolism and ritual, while mass humanity struggled against ignorance.

Communities, intentional neighborhoods created by beings desirous of preserving our great visions of today are being formed all over the planet to help persons realize people are related to one another.

The same truths spring eternally into world religions and life experiences. Our dreams and our myths whisper much the same message. Persons aligned to life perceive the struggle of earth to survive.

As a being of other dimensions slips through the doorway to human form there is the adjustment to be made that is seen in the beauty and clarity of the eyes of the newborn infant. Time and time again I've heard persons say, "See the wisdom on his face. If he could only talk." The infant gradually learns motor control, language, communication techniques and acceptable social patterns. In contrast, the Walk-in opens the door and is in the driver's seat of a new vehicle with all the wiring intact and gas in the tank. Where does he/she start?

The need to recapture a sense of identity and security is profound. The pain of expanded awareness causes one to deny, to try to shut down all the inflowing information. The unwanted bombardment of perception creates pain similar to a bright light thrown on when you have been sitting quietly in the dark. The blinding flash totally disorients you. The experiencing of such an expanded view of life causes you to grab with both hands whatever can serve to stablilize your picture of life. These are often family, church, or ethical/moral codes. The initial reaction is to find a quiet, safe corner and hold still.

Only as I began to find stability in my own inner and outer life could I brave sharing a glimpse of this experience. Since 1958 I have been in the process of integrating physical and spiritual awareness. The pain and guilt of the first ten years were spent simply trying to gain acceptance of myself . . . to find a safe place within myself. Only in this way could I figure out how to give my message without destroying my integrity. Repeatedly, I was reminded of the Bible quotation which says ". . . neither cast ye your pearls before swine lest they trample them under their feet and turn again and rend you."[21] This spoke to me of the caution I needed to use and of the preparation I needed to make.

I have often said that an inability to recall our past lives is God's mercy. Not remembering is a help. When one is finally ready, usually behind the veil of meditation or dreams, the experiences of the past are revealed. The same lack of past life memory is a blessing for the newly arrived Walk-in soul. If the changeover is discovered too soon this new one could be destroyed. Realize that the life opportunity offered to the Walk-in is fraught with hardship or the preceding inhabitants would not have been so willing to release it. If the incoming one were abruptly confronted with past life recall, he/she would rarely be able to handle

---

[21]Matthew 7:6.

the assault. Time is necessary to pull together the courage needed, as well as the connection with the higher dimension of mind. Imagine the delicate work of self-healing, sorting out the available options and fulfilling previous responsibilities. The new arrival needs a protective and supportive environment as all sensitive and caring individuals do, but even more so while the vehicles are knitting. After the frequencies are well synchronized, the energy of the powerful soul flows outward, providing a positive charge that limits the amount of damage so easily done by criticism and attack.

Only great necessity will cause persons who have visionary spiritual knowledge to step forward. To share gently, privately, inconspicuously, has been the only way mystics have survived over the centuries. Even then most have experienced ridicule, rejection and hostility. Today the message comes, "Speak up. This is why you're here. Dare to be." For a brave and courageous soul this is the time. And for those ready to hear and to know, it is also your time. History will record humanity's choice.

Creative consciousness moves and flashes through the universe like phosphorus in the water of night. Today I let it sparkle and speak through my personality . . . tomorrow it will be through another. Lives are snuffed out daily; deeds are recorded in the history of the Great Life. Neither your struggle nor mine will stop the Cosmic Life. Noble concepts are created to help human minds deal with the "Great Life." From the flash of lightning that illumines one mind for a brief time, Divine laws, cycles, rhythms and teachings point humanity in the direction of greater comprehension of Truth. If enough people can receive but the reflection of this illumination, life may take a profound leap forward today. It will occur if humanity will listen to souls working sincerely as the messengers for our time.

The symbol of a golden age is held before us, encouraging us to believe, hang on, move carefully around the mountain's edge, because one slip and the abyss awaits. The human mind, once animal, received into itself the divine spark and started this ascent. It will not be wiped out. It can be pushed down, tortured, made to wait aeons of time. Humanity has glimpsed divinity. Already some have achieved it. The group mind, collective consciousness, has thrilled with the ecstasy of ascent. The same sexual attraction that draws male and female together is at work everywhere creating and recreating. Humanity and divinity have had intercourse. That connection will last in the imprint of human possibilities and though devastation wrecks havoc on all creation, the moment will come again.

Powerful moments I have tried to share with you. I am a private person, who forever wonders why I do this yet I have come to realize that to share with you my innermost self is my nature, just as the bird sings its song, the rose shares its fragrance, the sun shines its light. I open my reality to you because I must.

Humanity, you are my baby, my child, my lover, my reason for being. So, I offer these thoughts, my gift to be accepted in the spirit and understanding of your heart.

Section V
Astrological-Numerological Data

Chapter 22

In Support Of The Walk-in Experience

Many believe that significant events show themselves in the stars. Since ancient times persons have used the art of astrology to determine influences affecting individuals. I believe it's important to understand that these influences provide us with challenging circumstances as well as favorable conditions in which to make our choices. Outside influences such as the movement of planets create an atmosphere of a particular type or setting; our own astrological configuration is either supported or deterred within that framework.

A major teaching is that these influences cannot impel us to do anything, but we may feel compelled and thus act. The more aware we are of the energies influencing us, the more control we can have over our lives.

If an astrology chart is the story of the personality it will, in fact, continue to work for the Walk-in. It is the opportunities and the challenges of the personality. It records the weaknesses and strengths with which to work.

One soul will make use of this set of tools one way; another soul will use those influences differently. The Walk-in takes the chart, the strengths or weaknesses of the personality, and tries to use them in an opportune way. Think about babies born at the same moment. The results of their lives will be different even though the similarities will be striking.

Accordingly, an evolved soul will make the most of each opportunity. A lesser evolved soul will respond to a less evolved level. Thus, the astrological chart of the basic personality continues to work, even though the soul has changed, just as the body is of a particular sex and the incoming soul continues to work through it. The body and personality continue to serve as containers for the new soul to animate.

"The descent and re-ascent of the Monad or Soul cannot be disconnected from the Zodiacal signs!!"[22]

As a result of my understanding of astrology, and my curiosity about the possibility of a Walk-in exchange registering in a chart, I have included here the work of three astrologers approaching the event from different modes.

If you are interested in Astrology, I think the following studies will prove interesting. There are several different charts involved. I'd like to point out the natal chart of a native is the usual chart used for the study of one's personality and potential.

Horary Astrology is the name given to the study of an event chart. Such a chart is used here for the death experience. Also, especially significant to me, were the powerful realizations that came with the blessing of Herakan Baba (Babaji) at Haldwani, India. So, I have included an event chart for that occasion.

It is taught that Scorpio in a native's chart gives us some ideas of areas wherein one might be tested. Scorpio, we learn from Alice Bailey,[23] channels energy to us from cosmic sources. We have a second ray energy influence in the energy of Scorpio that pours to earth from Sirius. Sirius is related to Scorpio and we are told that the Sirian Logos is the Solar Angel of our Solar Logos.

In many esoteric writings we are told humanity is being guided by great ones from Sirius. "Sirius is the star of initiation . . . earth's hierarchy is under the spiritual direction of the Hierarchy of Sirius."[24]

---

[22]*The Secret Doctrine*, Vol. II (Adyar Edition, 1938).

[23]*Esoteric Astrology* (New York: Lucis Publishing Co.).

[24]*Symphony of the Zodiac*, Torkom Sarydarian (California: Aquarian Educational Group, 1980).

Thus, when Scorpio influence is powerful one can be given a great chance for initiation, growth and service. Humanity is currently being given opportunity as a whole for entering into the path of discipleship through Scorpio. Some individuals in their particular life pattern find the tests and challenges clearly marked by Scorpio's presence.

In the various charts you will note the powerful Scorpio interplay.

As I collected data to share with you, my readers, I felt it would be of interest to ask my friend, astrologer and numerologist, Ms. Barbara Everett, to review the chart and share her insights. Barbara is a well-known teacher and counselor in the Minneapolis area. In this chapter she will share a comparison of pertinent charts.

Also, I had met a lovely lady in Atlanta during a healing seminar a couple of years ago, after which she expressed an interest in the event chart of the Near Death Experience. Since my daughter was born during those minutes her birth chart is also the "exchange" chart. Ms. Judy Goodwin of Atlanta used the Sabian Symbols as a tool to gain insight to the experience. This, too, is included for your interest. Judy Goodwin is a licensed astrologer and psychic in Atlanta. Her readings include interesting variations including reincarnational histories and 90-year life cycle charts.

A third woman, known for her profound understanding of Esoteric Astrology, as well as being most knowledgeable in Spiritual Philosophy, is Joleen DuBois of Sarasota, Florida. She is a professional astrologer, minister and director of the Association for Aquarian Education, a New Age study group. She has studied the various charts and introduces exciting insights.

As you will see from the following pages each of the astrologers have approached the study and interpretation of the charts in a different mode. As I see this, it is no wonder people question the validity of astrology with its many aspects and approaches yet each one of these came to many of the same conclusions through the different ways. I hasten to add no one saw the work of the others, but each proceeded in the manner most comfortable for herself. As well, none have read the manuscript and the personal feelings it contains. So as I compile the contributions I see how well the material submitted acknowledges my feelings at the various times designated.

I think astrologers and numerologers will find the ladies have developed some exciting guidelines useful in studying the charts of the twenty-three million people who are estimated to have come critically close to death. Of this number some eight million are believed to be "experiencers" of the something "more." Often in these lives, these experiences have vast spiritual significance. Here in this chapter we are tracing the happenings of one life that seems to have left a trail easily discernible through the occult sciences. Perhaps here are keys helpful to others as they ask, "Am I a messenger as well?"

I thank each of these women for their interest and contributions.

—The Author

Note: For convenience the balance of this chapter will be divided into the following categories:

      A. Basic Astrology and Numerology
      B. Esoteric Astrology
      C. Sabian Symbols

A. Basic Astrology and Numerology

Barbara Everett Comments:

In the teachings of Astrology, each life is seen as a facet of God, shining through the Sun Sign to the degree of clarity that the individual is able to manifest. Each person advances towards the realization of his/her Sun Sign according to the people, circumstances, and events which formulate the life. We become a summation of our life process, and the energies of the sun, moon, and planets in our solar system either enhance or challenge the life plan.

In the case of a Walk-in, a more evolved soul replaces the original soul, but the chart itself must also be in cooperation with the incoming purpose in order for the plan to work.

In the case of Carol W. Parrish, Carol was born with the Sun in Aquarius, the Moon in Leo, and a Piscean Ascendent. Aquarius is a Fixed Air Sign, giving the person an inclination toward adventurous thought patterns, a strong sense of will, a need for freedom, an ability to work with groups, and a love of humanity.

The Moon in Leo, a Fixed Fire Sign, opposite the Sun sign, would indicate a pattern of strength and leadership from the past, increasing the determination of the person, sometimes to the point of stubborness.

When the Sun and the Moon are in opposition, there is a conflict of mind/emotions present within the person. Emotions can be very strong, and must be dealt with or the fire of the Leo is turned inward, causing physical distress and depression.

The Piscean Ascendent, a mutable water sign, increases emotional, spiritual and psychic sensitivities, sometimes to the point of pain. The person often is super-sensitive, almost like a sponge, absorbing the emotional discomfort of others.

Being born as an Aquarian, one of Carol's missions in life was to move out of the limitations of the past (Pisces) and forward into a new, more enlightened future. However, this mission was definitely complicated by the Sun-Moon opposition, which necessitates the balancing of the male/female parts of the self in order to make progress. In addition, the overly emotional and sensitive personality level, reflected by the Piscean Ascendent, made any moves forward nearly impossible. Young Carol's formative years reflected these various struggles, with competitive influences (Sun opposed Moon) involving her and her family. The psychic sensitivity was apparent at an early age (Piscean Ascendent) with the urge to be religiously "good" and always within the law of the church.

Prior to the time of the soul exchange, Carol was in dire emotional, mental, physical and spiritual distress. The present was too painful, the future hopeless, the strong pull of Pisces luring her back into the safety of oblivion. Perhaps it was the strength of the Sun/Moon opposition which allowed the transition to take place, the indomitable will of the two fixed signs which kept the physical heart (Leo) and the mind (Aquarius) "alive" in order for the soul exchange to occur, rather than to succumb to death (Pisces).

At the time of Carol's Near Death Experience, the Sun was in Scorpio, the sign of transition, birth and death, the sign of transformation. It is the sign of intense and deep inner power and awareness. In Carol's natal chart, Scorpio rules the house of birth/death and transformation. This sign then became the doorway for the exchange. The ability of the Scorpio influence to transform itself again and again, in spite of, or because of, tremendous challenges is a constant revelation to all.

Also note the Jupiter influence present. Usually we read Jupiter as "expansion" and call it a beneficent influence. Let's realize Jupiter could have been a protective or a beneficent influence offering the opportunity of a great service, great challenge or change. It will be interesting to watch the Scorpio and Jupiter combination there, within charts of other Walk-ins.

In the death process, we are reborn, and so it was for Carol, as the timid woman, reflecting more Piscean qualities than Aquarius, moved out of the hopeless struggle into peace and security, and an evolving Carol moved forward to activate the chart that was meant for a person dedicated to using authority, freedom and unusual mind abilities, tempered by compassion, sensitivity and great intuitive abilities.

The natal astrology chart seems more fitting to Carol of the present than of the past. Possibly the first soul was overcome by the power of the chart that it had chosen to work with, but kept it going long enough to realize the tre-

THE EXCHANGE
(Event Chart #1) Compared to Carol's Natal Chart

Natal:
Jan. 21, 1935
9:15 a.m. CST
Nettleton, Ark.
90' W 35 Long.
35 N 49 Lat.

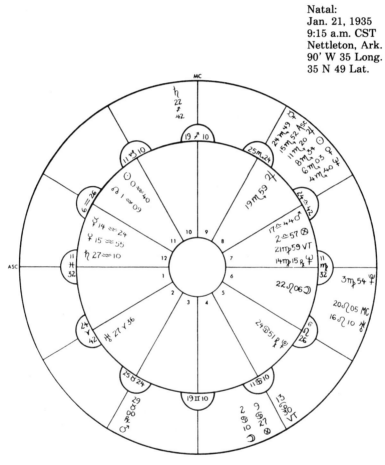

Event:
Nov. 1, 1958
7:20 a.m. EST
Clearwater, Fla.
82' W 47 Long.
27 N 58 Lat.

mendous possibilities before relinquishing it into the safe-
keeping of a soul better prepared to carry on the mission.

An interesting second event chart is the blessing by
Babaji at Haldwani, India. Fortunately Carol looked at her
watch and we are able to look at the influences active at
that exact time. This chart proves increasingly important
in the days and weeks afterward as memories bombard
Carol and more of her life work is revealed.

In the Event Chart from Haldwani, India, the Ascendent, Sun, and Moon are conjunct in Libra, emphasizing the
shift of personality levels from the emotional essence of
Pisces to the mental essence of Libra. Libra is the sign of
justice, both ethical and merciful, evenly balanced between
mind and emotion. Libra encompasses the ability to bring
harmony to opposing factions, those within self, and those
between people and/or ideals. It is the arbitrator, the one
who listens, learns, speaks and then reveals the law through
mercy and justice.

At this memorable point, the soul and personality of
Carol were then evenly balanced with her life's purpose.
The on-going conflict within the self of mind and emotion,
so evident in the natal chart with sun opposed moon, blend-
ed together to permit a larger glimpse of the total plan was
only the beginning, and the journey continues to be revealed as Carol herself is prepared.

For many people with a strong Libran influence, decision making is often a perplexing dilemma. However, in
Carol's case, also having Saturn in Libra in the 12th House
would increase her ability to be decisive. This need is evident in her natal chart with Saturn also posited in the 12th
House in Aquarius. Saturn works particularly effectively
in both Aquarius and Libra, being co-ruler of Aquarius,
and exalted in Libra. With Saturn in the 12th House in
both charts, a decision of dedication to humanity would
have been an obligation from the past, a promise to be part
of the evolving Plan. It would have existed on a subconscious level (12th House) until the proper opportunity
presented itself to emerge.

THE BLESSING
(Event Chart #2) Compared to Carol's Natal Chart

Natal:
Jan. 21, 1935
9:15 a.m. CST
Nettleton, Ark.
90' W 35 Long.
35 N 49 Lat.

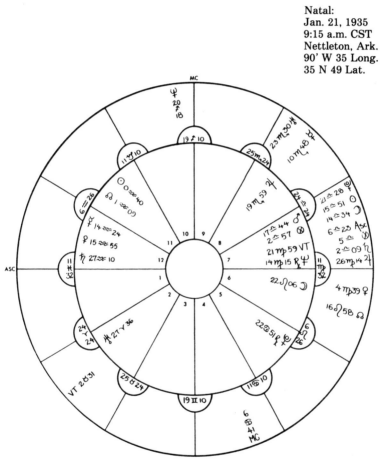

Event:
October 9, 1980
5:50 a.m. NST
79' E 31 Long.
29 N 13 Lat.
Haldwani, India

The Haldwani, India, chart also emphasizes the shift of another great personal challenge for Carol. Lilith, the point of greatest frustration or loss from the past, needing confrontation in the present, shifted from the intensely personal 2nd House of money, possessions, and value systems, to the 8th House. Here Lilith can be seen as the victory over mortal death, and the knowledge of continuity of life.

It seems evident that the first event chart began the transformation process with Scorpio so prominent, as life on all levels changed completely. The process was accelerated in the second event chart with the merging of personality and soul. Intensity became the by-word, and the focus was on the need for cooperation to bring forth ethical and spiritual changes.

It is interesting to note that this part of Carol's life and growth came to public attention in 1982 by the guides of Ruth Montgomery in her book *Threshold to Tomorrow.*

In January of 1982 I had cast a yearly chart for Carol, which put Scorpio on the ascendent for that year. This indicated that wherever Scorpio appeared in her natal chart would be high-lighted during that particular year. Scorpio, the sign of transition, transformation, is the ruler of Carol's eighth house of secrets. The secrets were transformed into revelations. Birth and death have been intimate companions of Carol's for many years, and during 1982 greater expansions of these modes of life would be "born" for the enlightenment of humanity.

As I also work with the study of NUMEROLOGY, I needed to satisfy myself as to how Numerology could work in conjunction with the concept of a Walk-in.

The esoteric teachings of Numerology open our understanding to the pattern of an evolving soul, its present incarnation and the challenges and expectations it will experience. Each person comes into being to perform a chosen task, a mission and a plan, carefully formulated by the Lords of Karma, the entering soul, and the compassion of the Universal God.

The plan is revealed through the Life Path, which is composed of the month, day and year of a person's birth. We are born at the time, place and in the circumstances most necessary for our advancement. Our plan is a culmination of what we have achieved up to the present, and what we can further achieve. We usually enter a Life Path not fully knowing how best to express that vibration, and it requires considerable time for us to merge comfortably with that plan.

In Carol's case, her birthdate of January 21, 1935, brought a vibration of 22/4. In the teachings, it is revealed that certain numbers carry additional potential, that they reflect the ability to be more creative, more influential, more powerful. The numbers 11, 22, and 33 are considered to be in a category reserved for the more adventurous and daring individuals. Often they are termed Master numbers, which describe the possibilities of high-level achievement. However, these particular numbers also carry with them heightened emotions, greater challenges and possibilities of burn out and disappointment.

Because these numbers are delicately balanced, the individual often must use the vibration at a lower frequency, an 11 becoming a 2, a 22 becoming a 4, a 33 becominng a 6, until the body/mind/emotional vehicle is more capable of maintaining the higher vibrations.

During Carol's early years, she was strongly influenced by the vibration of the number 1 from the January birth month. This number is very challenging for a child and young adult because it seeks to increase independence, personal resourcefulness, and decision-making. Often there is much loneliness and a feeling of isolation during this time. Later in life this vibration can be used more advantageously.

As each person progresses through life, the Life Path becomes a beacon, drawing them forward to express that vibration more completely. The 22/4 Life Path of Carol's was a great challenge, carrying the potential for serving humanity, creativity of thought, expansion of consciousness and an idealistic vision for mankind.

Given her early sensitive nature, the 4 vibration became the level that Carol chose to use because it carried more security, form and continuity than the high-powered 22. Four is the number of discipline, of following through, of being the patient builder, more efficient and organized than creative and experimental. That solid, dependable vibration surrounded her in a secure (if rigid) pattern of life, of home, family, responsibility, of endless details and organization.

The soul exchange released the limited personality, who needed to be enclosed and protected (4) to the more expansive personality (22) who would willingly take risks, go beyond limitation, and eventually would be involved in shaping spiritual values for other eager aspirants.

We all begin to shift our pattern between the ages of 28 to 34, moving then to the influence of the birthday and also moving more fully into our Life Path. Shifting to the 21 (3) of her birthday, Carol became more expressive through her activities, her ability to share thoughts in an inspiring way, an impressive example of the 3 vibration. Eventually, this energetic vibration would lead Carol to lecturing, teaching, TV and radio work and writing. At the same time, she shifted into the higher vibration of the 22 Life Path, seeking to change the confinements of physical, emotional, mental and spiritual limitation of herself and others.

The 22 led to the more universal approach of life, away from the extreme emotionalism and personal dependence, to seeing life on a cosmic level, with ever-expanding possibilities.

This shift from a 4 vibration to a 22 vibration is more impressive than it may seem at first glance. It is akin to moving from the basement level of a skyscraper to the top floor on an express elevator, with the need to adjust immediately to the changing scene and altitudes. It is no wonder, then, that her family and friends were confused by the changes, as was her own personality, as it had to shift constantly to keep pace with the inner expansion.

The 22 is often the visionary, the mystic with practicality, one who can put ideas into form, who can participate creatively in the destiny of humanity. With that, of course, comes the challenge of continuing to function in a human form, to take care of the body, to relate to others, and still not relinquish the dream of what can happen for humanity with enough dedication, persistence and willing workers.

From Numerology we can observe the influences of both event charts. In 1958, Carol was experiencing a nine personal year. Nine is the completion of a cycle, a year of finish, often one of loss, especially for a person with little hope. It may even take the form of death. Its motivation is often to separate the person from personal affairs and instill higher aspirations and discrimination. But if one has not reached the understanding of such values, its expression is frustration, loss and despair.

The Universal vibration for that year was a five, the number of change, the ability to move towards greater understanding of human conditions. As a Universal vibration, its purpose was to awaken everyone to change within themselves and to expand their understanding of humanity in all lits variations.

The personal influence for Carol of the day of the death experience was a three, the vibration of joy and creative expression. Three is one of the most verbal, expressive and enthusiastic of vibrations, an outgoing, energetic demonstration of energy. On that day, despite the anxiety of the situation, Carol did find a joyous renewal of life, one which lifted her forever from the bitter aspects of fear and disappointment to the spiritual appreciation of life in all of its facets.

The Universal energy of that day was an eight vibration, the number of power, expansion and the ability to function simultaneously in the world of matter and in the world of spirit. It is often seen as the bridge to higher consciousness for those ready to take that step.

The year of 1980 was a 22/4 personal year for Carol.

Coinciding with her Life Path, it was a year of special significance for her. A 22 year evokes unexpected changes,
travel, rapid fluctuations of emotions, heightened potentials, the possibility of a creative breakthrough. Carol's
personal life that year was evidence of the powerful impact
of 22, culminating in her experience with Babaji in Haldwani, India. At that meeting the spiritual expectation of
the 22 Life Path began to emerge with more potential than
ever before.

The Personal Day was a five vibration, the energy of
change, the number of humanity, the number of understanding. The personal changes began then, and the expansion of the vision and goal for humanity took shape.

The Universal vibration of that day was a one, the energy of new beginnings, the life-force. The one vibration
signifies the birth of ideas, independence, influence, and
strength. How appropriate for the second event chart to
carry this vitality as its Life Path number.

In summation, these number vibrations helped the
drama to unfold for Carol's mission, and the role she is to
play in inspiring humanity. We each either cooperate or
deny the plan set before us. Fortunately, the events of 1958
helped to prepare Carol for the events of 1980. Cooperation
leads to satisfaction, denial to unhappiness. Each of us will
be remembered by the fruits of our life, and those of Carol
W. Parrish-Harra's life are still maturing, for herself and all
who hear her message.

—Barbara A. Everett*

B. Esoteric Astrology Data

Esoteric Astrology is a more advanced form of Astrology that is used to help give insights to the behind-the-
scenes activity of the soul in quite a similar manner as

---

*I have used Neil F. Michelsen's Emphemeris and hand calculated the mathe-
matics. The time and place of birth, the Near Death Experience, and the Blessing
in India were supplied by Carol.

mundane or exoteric Astrology addresses its translations to the study of the personality, its strengths, weakness and opportunities. At this time interest in this approach is expanding and Joleen Ayres DuBois has been noted for her vast understanding of this challenging approach. She frequently lectures and teaches in this little understood area of expertise.

Joleen A. DuBois comments:

The natal horoscope reflects a celestial portrait of a human soul's entrance into incarnation. It points out the starting point of human life and is a picture of certain Atomic (karmic) substances the Soul/Personality has to work with in this life pattern. The natal chart is then a symbolic portrait of energy. The responsibility for the correct usage of the energy, the atomic substance, belongs to the native of the horoscope.

Each year of life of the native corresponds to the progressions (forward movement) of the horoscope which ignite the potential, and help to define the cycles of experience which promote spiritual unfoldment. So, as the native grows, the horoscope progresses, bringing a correspondence and synthesis between the activities of the person and the planetary energies.

The astrologer/counselor must thoroughly acquaint himself with the potential outlines in the natal horoscope from a holistic viewpoint before the unfoldment of the progressive cycles can be understood. He must also acquaint himself with the past and present psychological attitude of his client to gain an accurate perspective of his spiritual and mundane achievements and future goals in order to synthesize the cycles.

I want to explain to you the astrological evidence that gives support and credence to Carol's Near Death Experience and subsequent Walk-in experience, confining myself to the astrological evidence that deals with that event. I will show you the natal potential, the corresponding pro-

Carol's Natal Chart Compared to the
Exchange (Event Chart #1)
with Secondary Progressions for Nov. 1, 1958

Tropical/Placidus
Geocentric
Jan. 21, 1935
9:15 a.m. CST
Nettleton, Ark.
90° W 35 Long.
35 N 49 Lat.

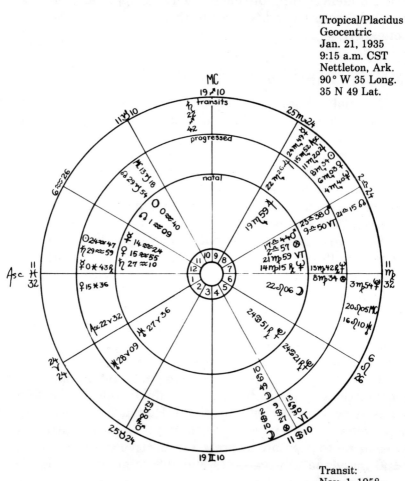

Transit:
Nov. 1, 1958
7:20 a.m. EST
Clearwater, Fla.
82° W 47' Long.
27 N 58 Lat.

gression, and the transiting cycles which ignited the experience.

The Sun was transiting (traveling) through the constellation of Aquarius at the time of Carol's birth. The Moon was in the Zodiacal sign of Leo, and Pisces was on the horizon (the rising sign). The Leo Moon in the sixth house suggests this life would be directed to service and healing through her heart or love nature. The Aquarian Sun (life energy) in the eleventh house indicates her service would be found in working with and organizing groups of people through a New Age Aquarian philosophy of brotherhood, unity and equality of human rights. In addition, it also indicates advanced Uranian thinking and methodology. Pisces rising reveals a mystical soul, a visionary prophet, with a senstivity to the masses. (Using the Esoteric approach to Carol's chart, the rising sign indicates these qualities will be used in her life work.)

The planet Uranus, "the awakener" is the exoteric ruler of her Aquarian Sun. It is found in the second house of spiritual and mundane resources and values brought in from a previous life time, and will be naturally expressed as an inherited gift. Uranus suggests her service will bring enlightenment to groups of people. By her own presence and radiance, she will reflect and ignite the spiritual-creative potential within those who are around her, magnifying their own spiritual resources. For is it not true, the saying, "What you see in others is a reflection of your own self?"

Jupiter, the planet of philosophy, religion and teaching, is found in the eighth house of mystery, death and transformation in Pluto's sign of Scorpio. This says Carol has an ability to teach the mystery/wisdom teachings, through philosophy and religion. It will also bring her into contact with death on a personal and impersonal level which can serve to transform her own life and the lives of others.

The Sun is the exoteric and esoteric ruler of her Leo Moon, found in the eleventh house of groups and associations. Since the Moon rules the immediate past life, it then suggests to me the preparation of her last life, (the Moon) was for the service she was to give in this life through her heart center, which could be expressed through spiritual healing, informing the public and teaching groups. To bring an understanding of "Aquarian Community" through selfless living and dedication to a higher plan for humanity, would be one of her eleventh house dreams.

Neptune, the planet of sacrifice, mysticism, and striving toward a closer union with the Divine, is the exoteric ruler of Pisces, in her seventh house of relationships and marriage. This suggests a life of sacrifice with a commitment to a relationship with others, to the building of a spiritual community, to form a contract between herself and the life mission (the rising sign) which would mean sacrifice to physical/social pleasures. It also reveals there can be much sacrifice and sorrow in the marriage experience.

Pluto, the planet of power, death and transformation, is the esoteric ruler of Pisces, her rising sign, found in the fifth house of love, children and creativity. It implies released power which will give birth to creative ideas, children, literature, art or culture. Pluto's contact to Carol's Aquarian Sun, found nestled between the axis of the fifth and eleventh house, shows there will be love given, received and taken away. It is through this experience of spiritual testing, which can bring a kind of death to the personality and ego, (the Sun) to expand her mission for the upliftment of others. Pluto is in the sign of Cancer, the energy of one's personal foundation, both spiritual and mundane, and Pluto will bring cycles of experience which will strengthen and resolve any past life (the Moon rules Cancer) karmic errors, to allow advancement in this life, enabling her to construct higher levels of consciousness and build a spiritual will.

The axis of the fifth/eleventh house is further emphasized through the pre-natal solar and lunar eclipses. January 5, 1958, a solar eclipse occurred in 13 degrees of Capricorn in the eleventh house, while a pre-natal lunar eclipse occurred January 19, 1958, at 28 degrees of Cancer in the fifth house of love, children and creativity, con-joining Pluto, the planet of death and transformation. This suggests through the progressive cycles of planetary ener-gies, that much attention will be given in the department of groups, associations, love, creativity and death. You will see the importance of the pre-natal solar eclipse in the Near Death event chart.

Finally, returning to Pluto, notice the tension contact that planet makes to Mars, forming in astronomical lan-guage, an applying square of 83 degrees. My own experi-ence has seen these powerful tension aspects in the charts of very creative and spiritually advanced people. The older books of astrology seem to see the square aspect in way which would scare most of us, giving a sense of defeat. Yet as the world grows, and humanity evolves, astrology ex-pands as well in her understanding. So, this planetary con-tact releases great power to develop spiritual will and higher states of awareness through intense trials and Near Death Experiences. Mars, the planet of personal drives and ambitions, is in the sign of balance and justice. This can also be seen as cause and effect, Karma. The sign of Libra.

Moving into the first event chart, the Near Death Ex-perience/Exchange Chart, taking place on November 1, 1958, at 7:20 a.m. EST in Clearwater, Florida, I have used for my interpretation the secondary progression for that data and the transiting event chart.

At first glance, I observed the heavy emphasis of transiting planets in the eighth house. This suggests an experience which would have a major transforming effect, and any decision made during this time frame would also be made from the very depths of her being.

The next point of interest is the progressed Midheaven. The Midheaven refers to experience which can bring great life changes, a point some astrologers refer to as destiny. Carol's natal Midheaven is in the sign of aspiration, Sagit-tarius, to reach toward higher and greater goals through philosophical and spiritual striving. Its exoteric ruler is Jupiter (having a special relation as the esoteric ruler of the

Aquarian Sun) written about earlier in this commentary. The esoteric planetary ruler of Sagittarius is the Earth, emphasizing a one-pointed effort through an earthly mission, serving as an "awakener" for humanity—or as a Light Bearer—showing the way of the spiritual path to others, through love and creative ideals (the Earth is in the fifth house). Sagittarius is the seeker of higher truths. The progressed Midheaven for November 1 is found at 13 degrees of Capricorn at the exact point of the pre-natal solar eclipse. This reveals the potential for a crisis which could have brought a change in her life and direction.

The progressed Ascendant has moved to Mars-ruled Aries, the sign of the pioneer, the blazer of new paths and ideas. Mars is still in square aspect to Pluto, the energy of trials/testing, and Near Death Experiences, and is "kicked" into action through the progressed Sun, making a mathematical angle of 150 degrees, or the inconjunct to Pluto. This aspect is always seen in a death chart, physical or psychological, and also indicates the opportunity for redirection, or initiation into another state of consciousness, through crisis. Certainly there will be a change in the personality ego, (the Sun) which can reconstruct the ego's foundation (Pluto in Cancer). The progressed Moon is in the sign of emotions and family relationship changes, and is ready to enter the fifth house of love and birth, bringing experience and change in that department.

That period of crisis began when transiting Mars (ruler of the progressed Ascendant of Self), formed the tension aspect to the planet of karma, fear, coldness and depression (Saturn in the natal horoscope). Saturn, the planet some refer to as the "Grim Reaper," if handled properly during its tests, will also lead to spiritual reward.

Transiting Mars, in September 1958, was at 29 degrees of Taurus, a position within the great cluster of fixed stars called Pleiades. In the wisdom teachings it is said to have a mythical relationship to the World Mother who gives birth to advanced beings. In mundane astrology the Pleiades is given a keyword of the "Weeping Sisters," and indicates an experience associated with sorrow. Transiting Mars is in the third house of communication, the immediate environment and relationships. Found there, it suggests that the mundane cause of the pain, depression and sorrow came through an environmental relationship, perhaps within the family. When Mars turned retrograde, it moved away from Saturn, leaving Carol in a state of preparation for decisions about her life. On November first it moved back to its direct contact to progressed Saturn, which brought the clinical death, separation of the soul from the physical body, allowing for the change of consciousness.

Let's now look at the contacts the progressed and transiting planets were making to the natal Midpoints (a so-called half-sums) which further supports the Near Death Experience. Mid-points are marked by the half-way positions in the Zodiac between two points, or planets. They help to further support and synthesize the previously given conclusions.

Looking first to the transiting planets, we see the transit Moon is in opposition to the natal mid-point of Venus/-Jupiter indicating the event saw the birth of a child, as does the transiting Sun in square aspect to the Midpoint of Jupiter/Uranus. Transit Mercury opposing the Midpoint of the natal Moon/Saturn, suggests, as so many other of the Midpoint contacts (which I will not point out for the sake of space, time and repetition), the thoughts of separation and taking leave of this physical incarnation (body). Transiting Neptune (ruler of the natal Ascendant and Self) is in conjunction to the natal Midpoint of Mars/Jupiter and shows an environmental relationship which seems fruitless or deceptive in some way. Mars is the planet of surgery, and Neptune, the planet that mundanely refers to drugs and poison, also points out a problematic experience dealing with surgery, connected in some way with drugs or anaesthesia. Transiting Pluto touches off a square to the natal midpoint of Jupiter and the Midheaven, indicating a great life and directional change.

The secondary progressions of the Sun square to the natal midpoint of Moon/Saturn again shows separation and intense personal trauma and pain. Perhaps this would also indicate a death wish. The progressed Ascendant squares the natal midpoint of Mars/Uranus, which indicates a personal upset, and surgery. At the same time the progressed Ascendant also squares the natal midpoint of Saturn and the Midheaven, bringing with it the potential for a separation from others, sorrow and life changes.

Finally, the transiting vertex point which deals with life circumstances and relationships is in 13 degrees of Cancer, with the anti-vertex point conjoining the pre-natal solar eclipse of 13 degrees of Capricorn, conjunct progressed Midheaven. This certainly promises life changes. The vertex point also conjoins the fixed star of Sirius, which the wisdom teachings say has a connection with the spiritual hierarchy. This can suggest through critical circumstances a crisis emerged, which may have released the present personality, to allow for the exchange with an advanced consciousness which would carry on the Earthly life mission.

Event Chart number two, which we have called the Blessing Chart, portrays the event in Haldwani, India. Carol's natal horoscope was advanced by secondary progression for October 9, 1980, with the transits set for 5:50 a.m. India time, in Haldwani, 79°31' East, and 29°13' North, latitude.

Jupiter and Sagittarius, and their great expansive energies rules foreign travel and spiritual pilgrimage. Its cycle may witness a reaching out to explore new idea, seek new meanings about life and a desire to gain new knowledge and wisdom. If accomplished, this cycle will manifest in a new sense of personal integration to be shared with others.

In Carol's natal horoscope, Sagittarius is found at the highest point in the chart at the Midheaven. When touched by cycles of progression it can bring experiences which will animate life changes—the "touch of destiny." On October 9, the transiting planet Neptune in Sagittarius was con-

Carol's Natal Chart Compared to Blessing (Event Chart #2) with Secondary Progressions for October 9, 1980

Tropical/Placidus
Geocentric
January 21, 1935
9:15 a.m. CST
Nettleton, Ark.
Secondary Progression
October 9, 1980

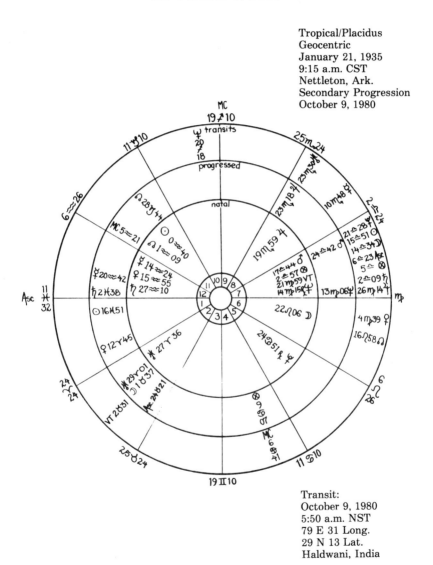

Transit:
October 9, 1980
5:50 a.m. NST
79 E 31 Long.
29 N 13 Lat.
Haldwani, India

joining the Midheaven, bringing with it an urge to seek the divine, a sense of holiness, changing spiritual values, as well as establishing new spiritual contacts and a feeling of exaltation. The "aura" of the whole Neptunian contact gives a sense of divine direction, traveling in spirit, or physically, to the "holy city" or temple. An increase in High Self perception and intuition is very likely. The challenge is to integrate all mystical, spiritual and physical experiences on an earthly level, such as the architect who puts his visions on paper and then must transfer them into form. Neptune experiences can remain a cloudly illusion or even a glamor, if not treated practically.

Jupiter is found transiting the seventh house of marriage, partnerships, and confrontations or encounters with others. I have noticed when Jupiter transits this house it can often find the native making a contact with his spiritual teacher (this is also true of the fifth house). Transit Jupiter is making a contact with the mid-points of Moon/Saturn and Sun/Neptune. This indicates a difficult journey, a spiritual blessing and/or a point of achievement, spiritually or mundanely. Transiting Jupiter also contacts the midpoint of the Moon's Node/Neptune indicating an occult meeting with one who can have a transforming affect on Carol, one who will reflect her own great spiritual beauty. This contact would be karmic in nature and of positive expression and likely to be repeated in some manner in her next incarnation.

A critical contact is made with transit Uranus, ruler of Carol's birth Sun (in Aquarius). T. Uranus is in conjunct to secondary progressed Jupiter (co-ruler of the rising sign), and is approaching a 90 degree angle (square) to her natal Saturn. This critical contact can bring opportunity for a spiritual awakening, a blessing, which breaks through the karmic bonds of a past life releasing her to face the future with new ideas, visions and for expanding horizons for humanity in a selfless manner.

Saturn in Carol's natal twelfth house at birth suggests she brought in subconscious feelings of personal fear, inadequacy about herself, feelings of oppression and bringing a strong need for solitude, or at least a strong sense of being alone. If she developed her spiritual inclination and sense of religious values (twelfth house), it was likely to see a change, or at least a turning point between the ages of 26 and 29. It is possible the blessing from Babaji may have released the balance of that karmic bondage.

The secondary progressed Moon is in a separating square to Carol's natal Sun, and had been since August of 1980. This cycle suggests stressful challenges which deal with both past, present and future. Children, family, love ties and personal dreams are likely to be involved. These experiences would confront Carol's basic spiritual and moral fibers, causing her to pull on all past resources for balance. The challenge would be for her to remain centered and keep her attention on the future while the emotionally uprooting events tear away at her foundation and values. (It was during this period Carol's daughter and grand-daughter made their physical transition and moved to a higher state of consciousness.) At the time of this event, transiting Uranus was square to her natal Leo Moon, a cycle which often sees swift and unexpected changes, profound emotional upheaval, a releasing of loved ones, friends and groups. (Astrologers, note Moon ruled Cancer is located on the fifth house of children, indicating this event would likely involve love relationships and offspring).

Finally, the Secondary Sun has progressed to 16° and 51' of Pisces. In 1975 and 1976 the progressed Sun had crossed her rising sign bringing about experiences which could have put her into the beginning phases of her life's work, the development stage. On the day of Carol's meeting with Babaji in 1980, the P. Sun made a contact with the midpoint of Venus/Mars bringing about opportunity for a spiritual or physical marriage, perhaps the mystical marriage . . . union or fusion of Personality and Soul.

The degree symbol for her progressed Sun, according to Isidore Kozminsky:

"Under the influence of the Sun. A gaudily dressed officer holding aloft a spear of gold. Denotes one of magnetic force, patience, and determination who wins his way by sacrifice of self for the sake of his ambition and who will never rest until he has achieved his purpose. He is identified with a great cause or a great production, spreading knowledge or giving pleasure. It is a symbol of Announcement."[25]

—Joleen Ayres DuBois*

C. Sabian Symbol Data

The Sabian Symbols method appoints a visionary value to each of the degrees of the Zodiac. To study a chart one researches the significant degrees (planet placement, etc.) and reads the story being woven by the dramas revealed. The method became increasingly popular as an appreciation of the work of Carl Jung grew. The symbols are often used in terms of contemporary psychology, philosophy and astrology.

Judy Goodwin comments:

To begin to see the esoteric significance of events, I use the Sabian Symbols (SS), reflecting clairvoyant Elsie Wheeler's visions on the meanings of the 360 degrees of the Zodiac. Dane Rudhyar's *An Astrological Mandala* is my source for synthesizing the symbology in light of planetary interaction. The SS for the Ascendant of your Near Death chart, 28° Scorpio, is "an Indian Squaw pleading to the chief for the lives of her children," (p. 209) symbolic of your learning that you had much work to do still on earth includ-

---

[25]*Zodiacal Symbology and Its Planetary Power*, Isidore Kozminsky (Arizona: Tempe. A.F.A. Inc.).

*I have used a TRS-80, model I computer, with the M-65 program, designed by Matrix software, to calculate the mathematics. The time and place of birth, along with the time and place of the Near Death Experience information and Blessing in India was supplied by Carol.

ing family responsibilities, and so must return. The Scorpio energies of this chart work through Pluto in Virgo, for which the symbolic reading, "Black and white children play together happily," (p. 152) shows that your work (Virgo) would be central to the transition into the humanitarianism of the Aquarian Age. Viewing these Scorpio planets individually, we see that this work required a period of transformation of your faith (Neptune), values (Venus), will (Sun), philosophy (Jupiter) and consciousness (Mercury) which took 22 years, significant in light of the fact that you are on the 22 Life Path Numerologically, that of the Master Builder; your natal Moon is 22° Leo, and Saturn in the Near Death chart is at 22° Sagittarius, promising 22 years in which you expand your wisdom. When it was time for your next major step, the moments naturally had to stimulate one another Astrologically and Numerologically, because the balance of the universe is measured by these sciences.

Both major angles, the Midheaven (MC) and the Ascendant of the Near Death chart were activated by the planets during the Blessing. In addition to Mars crossing the Ascendant, Venus was Conjunct the MC at 4° Virgo, describing the public meeting with Babaji whose blessing revealed the further unfoldment of your path to you, and fulfilling the natal suggestion of your Twelfth House Aquarian Venus, the attraction of spiritual friends at a public gathering. The SS for this conjunction aptly describes not only the aim (MC) of the Near Death Chart, but the result of the Blessing: "A man becoming aware of nature spirits and normally unseen spiritual agencies" (p. 153). Saturn crossing into the Eleventh, the house it co-rules with Uranus which is Conjuncting Mercury, the messenger, in the Near Death chart, describes the timing of a sudden change in the nature of your understanding of the karma of your Near Death event. The SS for Saturn's placement at 2° Libra reflects this: "The dawn of a new day reveals everything changed." (p. 173)

The Blessing chart's MC at 11° Cancer is exactly trine

the Near Death chart's Jupiter at 11 Scorpio (as well as
your natal Ascendant), with Jupiter, planet of growth and
spiritual development, falling in the Near Death chart's
Tenth House—a double statement of the aim of both
events being the expansion of your spiritual career. The
Near Death occurred a month before your Jupiter Return,
a time of philosophical new beginnings, and since your
natal Jupiter is in Scorpio by house and sign, for you new
beginnings develop from crises. At 26° Virgo in the Blessing chart, Jupiter is also the focal point of a Yod, the
"Finger of God" aspect, between your natal Saturn and
Uranus, rulers of your Aquarian Sun, reinforcing the message that it was time for you to adjust your life once again
so that another period of growth could unfold. A second
Yod was formed by transit to your natal chart during the
Blessing, with the transiting Sextile between Jupiter in
Virgo and the Mars-Uranus Conjunction in Scorpio Quin-
cunxing your natal Second House Uranus in Aries. This
Yod triggered the many adjustments prefacing your beginning a new life with new values to establish for yourself
and those with whom you would come to work, live, learn
and grow.

   Mar's Seventh House placement and the heavy Scorpio
emphasis in the Near Death Chart show that the action
would involve other people, which promise is fulfilled by
the Libran, cooperative emphasis of the Blessing chart,
and the fact that the two charts' Mars are in opposition, cooperating to tear down and rebuild as the Socrpio-Taurus
polarity defines. The keynote of the Blessing chart is "balanced action toward change" with the Libran Sun, Moon
and Pluto Conjunction in the First House describing a
change occurring in your conscious will (Sun), emotions
and home (Moon), here working together to transform your
value system (Second House), thinking (Mercury), friend-
ships and group goals (Uranus), and desire to act (Mars).
Pluto's exact Conjunction to the Libran North Node in the
Near Death chart unleashes the balancing intuition of the
Blessing, symbolized at 21 degrees by "a child giving birds

a drink at a fountain," which Rudhyar further defines as "a spontaneous, naive rapport at the spiritual level of pure feeling." (p. 186) Note that the North Node in both event charts, like in your natal chart, is in the Eleventh House, domain of the Aquarian Age.

The SS for the MC of the Blessing chart describes the aim of that moment: "A Chinese woman nursing a baby whose aura reveals him to be the reincarnation of a great teacher." (p. 117) The keynote according to Rudhyar is "revelation." Babaji thus, in that moment, nurtured the unfoldment of your new direction as a Messenger, Builder and Healer.

Your Light Experience remains a stable memory and source of inspiration as Neptune, planet of visions, is symbolized, "A massive rocky shore resists the pounding of the sea." (p. 194) Through its conjunction to Venus, SS "Deep Divers" (p. 195) it led you through an in-depth study of human nature and causality, until your will, reflected by the Sun, became motivated by the desire to regenerate through healing—SS, "A dentist at work." (p. 197) Neptune crossed your natal MC during the Blessing to announce that the period of study had culminated and it was time for you and your partners (natal Neptune in the Seventh House) to begin the move that Saturn, natural ruler of the MC, promised from its First House position in the Near Death chart: "A group of immigrants as they fulfill the requirements of entrance into a new country." (p. 223) Thus the karmic task you have chosen is to help lead people into a new stage of spiritual experience, further symbolized by Uranus in the Ninth House of the Near Death chart, SS, "A volunteer church choir singing religious hymns." Which is where your growth has led you ever since!

Although my focus was on the two event charts, the significance of the natal transits and progressions deserves an essay in itself. But the correlation between your being on the 22 Life Path and there having been 22 years between the two events which most drastically changed your

life were such a thought provoking tribute to the logical
order of the universe that I couldn't resist researching
them in detail.

—Judy Goodwin*

---

*I used the Koch Table of Houses because having studied both Numerology
and Astrology, I find Koch's house system always best reiterates the astrological themes numerologically. I worked from the Tropical Zodiac and erected
and interpolated the chart by hand.

Each of these persons continues to be interested in clues as to the identification of Walk-ins. If you have information to share, please write:

Barbara Everett
901 W. Minnehaha Pkwy.
Minneapolis, MN 55419

Chapter Chairperson Spiritual Frontiers Fellowship, Minneapolis/St. Paul; National Midwest Spiritual Frontiers Fellowship Retreat Committee. Numerology Coordinator Sunsight Educational Center. Member American Numerology Association.

Joleen Ayres DuBois
2221 Bispham Road
Sarasota, FL 33581

Director and Founder of the Association for Aquarian Education, Inc. Member of the American Federation of Astrologers, member of the research division of the AFA, member of the Agni Yoga Society, member of the Planetary Citizens.

Judy Goodwin
914 Collier Road, NW
Apartment H-4
Atlanta, GA 30318

Metro Atlanta Astrological Society, Co-editor, *The Atlanta Astrologer* and *The Jupiterian*, 1979-80; International Society for Astrological Research; Aquarius Workshops, Inc.; Association for Research and Enlightenment.

Addenda

Addendum 1

Meditation Guidance

Dear Reader,

In the following pages I am sharing some selected meditation guidance I have gotten over the years. I believe these will have meaning for you and you will see how some of the thoughts I have shared were received.

May the ideas presented bless and inspire you to know even more clearly that there *is* a protective and loving Higher mind in whom we live and move and have our being. I believe the transformation process is that unveiling of the Holy One within us that is in perfect harmony with the Holy of Holies that guides all life.

Great love,

The Author

October 4, 1975

Trying to live an inspired life is one of the most difficult tasks presented to one on the earth plane. If you so choose this life you accept the difficulties that come with that choice. Aquarian Love is new and different; it is to grow in time to be unconditional. Certainly no Love of the past has been like this. New awareness comes and all those seeking to pour Love through to the plane must serve. Some will serve with restriction, some will serve unknowingly, but for those who can and must and will, there will be service of the highest form, unconditional Love. Whether conscious of it or not, you are to give, my chela, for you are here of your choice and of mine. We are together to do this Love outpouring together. You are being most gently shown the path. You are stubborn and must be moved through difficulties so you can be more flexible for our use. Your greatest outpouring is ahead several years, not now. But the steps are now in action. Gently, let your head fall into our hands and give up the fears and separation, so we may guide more and more. Hold your leadership high. You are a foundation of hope. Let others try to destroy you and we will build you up. But within do not fear, for we and thee are one.

Few are called, truly. Some will choose to join you at great price. Why does it matter? The unfolding age is as certain as the morning. Your expression is just as certain. Let go of the fear and relax into the security and Love around you. Let the face relax, also the body, and accept into the physical that which is manifesting on every level. Shanti.

March 24, 1977

We are developing a householder tradition for the western world that is satisfying to the development of spiritually searching souls. The monastic system is exclusive; the Christian tradition for homemakers has become ineffective. A system of practices, private, yet communal in the sense of communion of souls, must be built. So, those needing guidance in the development of spiritual life will be helped to feel the Presence. It must become sustaining. Your expression is of this responsibility. The entire pattern of your personal life is to give you understanding to guide you in developing this concept. Take ten students and document their development. Use your own life to guide you and them in setting up guidelines. It takes inspiration and struggle. The seeker brings the pain and struggle. You are to supply the inspiration. Teach devotion as a strengthening force.

June 1978

Psychologists exploring consciousness are building the link between materialism and spiritual awareness. This is the bridge contributed by our time.

Spiritual teachers do not speak the language of academia nor do they desire to operate according to that discipline.

Scientists, the masters of materialism, were too limited to explore the abstract realm of thought. Beings of awareness have incarnated to bridge that gap. Most are dedicated aspirants passing a personal test (initiation) to become disciples by the work of their lives. Appreciate them.

November 2, 1978

The Path of a disciple is the expanding process that inner space starts in order to shatter all our dogmas, doctrines, separations, divisions, man-made laws, feelings, political ideas and thought forms.

There will be one humanity, one world, one brotherhood . . . no limitations.

The energy of freedom does not lead us first to happiness—it leads us first into great conflicts, changes and destruction of old patterns. Through pain, struggle and growth, we make change. The real fiery changes are the Path.

June 16, 1979

What difference does it make what name I give you as I speak to you within your heart? We each wear many names. Even as I face you as Carol, I know you as others at the same time.

If I speak to you as Jesus you can elevate yourself as a great Christian in touch with the Lord and Masters of the kingdom of that path; if I speak to you as Mary you can call acclaim to self for being the channel of She who guides in Love.

If I say to you, be the humble servant of a scribe, can you do that?

I ask you, can you see the Christ within yourself and Life? It is the challenge, for until you do it the Christ within cannot awaken. If I say imagine the brightest Light Being you can image, what occurs within the self? Do you see it? If I say to you image the most beautiful woman and you give time for it to arise, you will see a creation of great beauty, a lovely woman with the graciousness of Love and Light about her. Likewise, if I say create the most strong and handsome man you can image, a picture will come to mind. Even if you begin by a thought of another living being, if held, it will alter and improve. From where do these images come? From the resources of your own consciousness they arise and only because from there, within yourself, do they exist. So it is with the hard-to-create Light Being. The exercise to create the Being of Light forces you to reach to that level of self where that awareness arises and calls it to action. When you reach to find the most lovely woman or the exemplar of masculinity you are sifting through yourself and finding the consciousness of which you know, even as you yourself pulled your personality into being.

July 10, 1980

Loving Self is understood most correctly if we realize that that which we love regarding Self excites us when found in others. The mirror that shines the light to us cannot do so unless there is Light with which to illumine the mirror.

Resentment grows toward traditions that reflect our pains and discontents. As we stand ready and look in directions for help and get the vinegar of Life we are disappointed. We want a tenderness that allows us to find the gentle spot within ourself. If we find the soft place within our Self we can deal more tenderly and encouragingly with Self while it grows. If we find no grace, mercy or love within, we brace even harder toward our ills. We cannot get well if we remain full of hatred and anger. In softening and forgiving Self in the Light of Tenderness, healing may find its place to begin.

Can you see the scribe overshadowing? Laugh at this. Is it not you? Am I not you, my child, created for my expression? If you take a piece of sculpture and give it form, all others seeing it will say, "She made it." Others will say, "Doesn't it remind you of her?" and some will say, "You can tell it is hers." Perceptive ones link us to our creations easily. We are thus linked to the God consciousness through the stream from which we have come.

November 24, 1980

Many earthquakes such as have occurred this weekend will occur in the next few years. So much and so many that great fear will grow among men. The major task of Children of Light is to hold their faith in this time. As one gives into fear he has returned to darkness. The testing time is to say, "I can walk on through the storm unafraid, knowing it is a tunnel from one time frame into another." It is not the end of the world; it is the end of a period and is dramatically demonstrated. At the end of the last period equally great was the opportunity to retreat into fear. Each age change presents equal opportunity for growth. To die unafraid is greater than to live cringing in fear. Boldness carries one forward if with good motivation and intent. It is the response to challenge that is being measured even more than actions at certain times. One could say it is the testing of realities within the framework of drama. How many dimensions of nature can be controlled through the co-working of heart and mind! The greater the consciousness, the greater the ability to stay true under stress and change.

January 15, 1981

When you come into the presence of a Great Being of Love it clarifies your own ability to Love. As you experience the ability to see more clearly, accept that energy as of God and do not judge it. The energy is of God and stepped down to you. The major question is what new awareness, clarity or purification happened within you as a result of the outpouring you received. You are the one offered the opportunity through the use of this blessing. What are you doing with it?

February 1981

Pull the cloak of Christianity close around you for ten years. After that time greater acceptance of one another will manifest among God's children. The challenges that come now are to be met with the protection of your heritage. In the future each one shall say "yea" to others and no man will think he rules the earth.

Allow yourself to be guided to the summit of experience and fear no evil for my rod and my staff will comfort you. Shanti.

August 18, 1981

Each individual is represented by a completed circle. A group of individuals becoming one, work as a community. Think of each cell trying to exist without nourishment from another. The cell will die. Humanity has tried to think, work and act as one cell operating alone. As long as it was single cell life this was possible. Now humanity is a complex organism and none of the cells can exist alone.

When one cell creates a wall and thinks to protect itself from the neighbor, both the self-centered one and the one left out weaken. To create a one world concept in the minds of humanity, the air, water and earth must be endangered because only then will lesser beings recognize the interdependency of all life.

When one thinks only of his own future, retirement, insurance, savings, comfort, storing food for self, feeding of his own children, and no other, one is creating the beserk cell that goes on to destroy humanity. This cell in a body is cancerous; in the community it brings contagion. This cell endangers the life of all for it runs away into the distorted pattern of believing it gains by domination. This thinking kills community and cooperation.

There is a place to turn. It is to the Christ within. If this happens today your guidance will be complete. If you choose not to hear this message, you choose to be caught unaware. It is your choice. If you join in the disciples of Christ in their holy work you will participate in the preparation for the years of famine and fear. You will co-work with the Divine and the Christ in the maintenance of Mother Earth and her children.

The Christ is recruiting helpers from humanity. If you choose to wait you will be left to your own amusements while the choice moves to another. "I stand at the door and knock" is a forever message. In one life it comes at one time, in another life another time. The largest numbers are offered the knock now. Many deny the knock. It is a passing choice. If you move past that point without response, the life will carry you away from that point of choice. It is well known you cannot go back in time. Why do you think the Christ will not seek out more willing workers? Now the readiness must be undertaken for too soon we will face our challenge. Humanity's challenge will arrive for it is deemed necessary for the cleansing to be. We only alert you to the preparation stage. How you respond sets your own pattern in motion. We will guide our own. Rejoice.

February 11, 1982

You have been guided to the energy center for it is to serve a holy purpose. The very energy of the earth given here will aid in the sustaining of physical life, food for spirit and energy contact with the one of Light who protects and guides you.

For centuries ones have been made aware of the holy ground under their feet. While charged in such a way many are cleansed and awakened to higher awareness. All people of all times need this force. It will be especially beneficial in the years fast upon us.

Know yourselves as children of earth to be nourished by earth as well as children of spirit. Matter must be blessed and dedicated to spirit; spirit must freely communicate with matter. Thus mother and father are one and the new can be born. This period is the travail of childbirth—the feared time yet anxiously awaited. The time when the new life on earth can begin. Such a vision is held by those who guide you, not fearfully, but tenderly. We would comfort you and help you through the experience of the agony. Rejoice.

July 29, 1982

Those of you attuned to a high and gentle mind of oneness realize all must live fairly or war continues. There is no
part of the earth fighting a war while other parts do not.
For these many years the earth has already been in its war-
ring cycle. When brother kills brother or cell kills cell, it is
war.

The earth is already at war. The guidance we would give
is to prompt you to be of such high mindedness and confidence that you do not draw yourselves into it. Let it be
elsewhere while you give it no energy.

Gradually you each are changing. Most are responding
to the cleanliness and richness of nature, and study well.
Those who study least, draw close together; the least are
the first to become contaminated by fear and doubt.

Embrace all projects with one mind. Those who hold
back, lose. Giving and receiving are so linked together that
only then can the best occur.

July 29, 1982

It is not the intention of the hierarchy to interfere with the tests of humanity. Our intention is to have contact with some believing ones so if, in fact, humanity cannot free itself from its pattern of vanity, greed, and love of materialism there will be some who will preserve seeds of the highly developed root races or human beings to re-seed the world.

The earth is being challenged to become the place of beauty that it can be and to rid itself of its destructive patterns of behavior and its extremes in expression. Human life, the guiding consciousness of the earth, works exactly the same.

August 1, 1982

In the challenges of the next months many persons will suffer. This is not to strike fear in you. We would not tell you if a great war was ready, for if it wasn't, fearful thoughts bring into being just as the rain cloud is pulled together. We tell you suffering of many kinds comes to help persons "need God," life hunger pangs. Economic suffering helps persons to know what really matters. Physical pain helps us know the blessing of good health. You need to see how rich the group consciousness is, how little it lacks, how good you have it, to draw more goodness to you.

As you rejoice in the daily goodness, smiles come, enthusiasm flows and a wave of fresh vitality is given with which to carry on.

To those who are truly mine, I daily say, "Rejoice."

November 1982

The lives of those most greatly concerned with materialistic endeavors will be the heaviest. If you choose to build
up your treasures on earth, prepare to be challenged. You
pit your strength against the strength of heaven. Many
have tried this, it cannot be done.

Humanity does not believe this. You, Humanity, call
yourself "awakened." Can you live in stewardship rather
than what you call "ownership"? You own nothing except
your body. It is yours because you created it to experience
the physical world and your life here is always dependent
upon maintenance of your creation.

One is always challenged to maintain his creations or to
release them to others. If others take part in the maintenance of a creation, it lightens the load. Persons drawing
through ideas and energies for the benefit of many are the
stewards. Ideas, buildings, inventions and philosophical
concepts are all gifts to the many. Your participation is
your stewardship. If you think any of these can be owned,
you are still ignorant.

Ignorance is thinking without illumination. The Light of
High Consciousness is not turned on. We rejoice in the
reaching for new insights. God is the source of the Light
drawn into dedicated lives. Stewardship is enlightened participation in the maintenance of that which you perceive as
good. When any creation no longer is good to you, no
longer give to it. It will die or be picked up by others who
are now ready to support it. Move on to your next area of
stewardship. Rejoice.

Addendum 2

Sparrow Hawk Mountain Sanctuary

SPARROW HAWK MOUNTAIN SANCTUARY
by Sig Lonegren
29 October 1982

Astronomy   *Sacred Geometry*   *Earth Energies*

This sanctuary has been designed, as so many pre-Protestant Reformation sacred encloseres were, to enhance the possibility of heightened spiritual awareness. There are three factors that seem to be found at sacred spaces like Stonehenge, Solomon's Temple, the Great Pyramid, Chartres Cathedral, the Aztec and Mayan Temples of Mexico and many other places where men and women went to become more aware of their closeness to their Maker. These factors are:

1. These temples are *oriented towards significant horizontal astronomical events* (think of the Summer Solstice Sun rising over the Heel Stone at Stonehenge, or Solomon's Temple being oriented to the East, so when the East Gate was opened—only the Lord could enter through the East Gate—the rising Equinox sun would illuminate the Holy of Holies at the back of the Temple).

2. These temples were constructed with certain repeating ratios, referred to as *sacred geometry*. For example, the Parthenon was constructed using a ratio called phi, or 1:1. 618. The Greeks called this the Golden Section, and it was the fundamental ratio that led to the perfection of their statues, vases, and buildings. The ratio of the Parthenon's height to its width is exactly 1:1. 618. For the

Greeks, phi was synonymous with beauty.

The Gothic Cathedrals employed another sacred geometrical form that is considered to be particularly Christian—the *vesica pisces*. It is created by making a circle
with a compass, then, using the same radius, put the point
of the compass at any point on the circumference of the
first circle, and create a second one whose circumference
goes through the center of the first. The *vesica* is the
saucer shaped figure formed by the intertwining circles.
Notice that the top half of the *vesica* creates what is called
the Gothic arch.

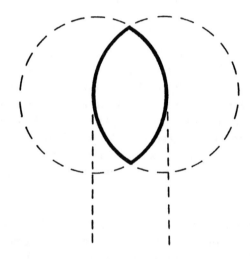

3. The third common theme found at all of these sacred
places is the notion that the ground itself is holy. We hear
this alluded to in the Old Testament when Moses encounters the burning bush. The Lord tells him to take off his
shoes because he is on *holy ground.* The Native Americans
of the southwest have the same notion in their sacred
enclosures they called kivas. These circular temples were
also constructed on holy ground or power centers.

Different cultures employ different techniques to determine where this holy ground is—where on the surface of
the earth to place their sacred enclosures. The tool that

most modern investigators are using is dowsing—the use of implements like the forked stick or a pendulum to determine things that would not ordinarily yield answers empirically, through the five senses. Most people may have heard of dowsing in terms of looking for water. And indeed, underground water is one of the manifestations of the Earth Mother that is found at every power center (holy ground). Ezekiel talks about this phenomonen when he tells us that a river of water "was issuing from below the threshold of the temple toward the east (for the temple faced east); and the water was (also) flowing down from below the south end of the threshold of the temple, south of the altar."[26]

Along with the water that is found at power centers, dowsers also find straight lines of male or yang energy they call energy leys. These are closely related to phenomena noted in Great Britain and in South America and other places where ancient civilizations built holy sites in straight lines. These lines come together like spokes on a wheel at especially sacred places like Stonehenge, and in Peru, at the Coricancha, the major temple of the Inca capital of Cuzco. These alignments of sites are called ley lines.

Astronomy, sacred geometry, and earth energy power centers; the Sparrow Hawk Mountain Sanctuary was designed with these three components in mind.

The front door of the sanctuary is oriented towards the setting sun on the equinox (both spring and fall). This means that when the front door of the sanctuary is open, the rays of the sun as it touches the western horizon on those two days will illuminate the altar and the cyclorama behind it.

The geometry of the sanctuary incorporates two basic sacred geometrical forms. The room itself is a rectangle that yields a ratio of 1:1. 618 width to length. This use of phi creates a sense of harmony and beauty in the propor-

---

[26]Ezekial 47:1.

tion of the room as a whole. Since the sanctuary serves as a vessel to carry the Light of Christ into the New Age, the Christian *vesica pisces* is an appropriate symbol to focus the attention on the altar and the power center that is underneath it. The *vesica* is created by a line on the flooring on one side, and the cyclorama on the other. In a sense, the cyclorama serves as a parabolic dish to focus these energies both on the altar and on the congregation.

The earth energies come together at the altar. There are two through energy leys, and a third one ends, or goes to earth, at the point of the altar. The water underneath manifests itself in what dowsers call a dome. Unlike surface water that is derived directly from rain, primary water comes from deep within the earth itself. (Perhaps it seeps there from fissures in the floor of the ocean.) In any event, it comes up under pressure through cracks in the rock, like the geyser Old Faithful, and ascends towards the surface of the earth until it hits an impermeable layer and then goes out laterally in other fissures in the rock as veins of water. From above, the dowser perceives this dome as roughly circular, with the veins exiting out, like legs on a spider.

The energy leys intersect over the dome. There are five veins of water that exit from the dome at the Sparrow Hawk Mountain power center. Four exit the sanctuary of the corners of the phi rectangle, the fifth exits out the front door.

Astronomy, sacred geometry, and the earth energies, these three concepts, when used in the construction of any sacred space, among other facets, will make for better meditations, increase the possibility of spiritual healing, and enhance the potential for heightened spiritual awareness. The Sparrow Hawk Mountain Sanctuary is a true sacred enclosure.

—Sig Lonegren

Solarcrete Construction Details

Developed by Solarcrete Corp., Erlanger, KY, the concept calls for the walls of a building to be a sandwich of expanded polystyrene (EPS) enclosed between layers of gunned on concrete. In our case, the styrofoam-like core of E.P.S. is 6" thick and the concrete 2½" thick on each side, reinforced with steel rebars and keydeck mesh. The rebars are tied together through the E.P.S. with special steel clamps to create a truss effect that results in an especially strong wall system. The other benefits are a super-insulated (R-26) wall, a very quiet sound transmission rating of 61, a seismic-3 rating, making the system appropriate for earthquake-prone areas, and a 2-hour fire rating.

The 8,000 sq. ft. Church and Seminary building was nearing completion when this photo was taken in March 1983. Its energy efficient walls have a 6" core of EPS foam sandwiched between layers of 2½" steel-reinforced concrete that was gunned on inside and outside. The steel rebars are tied together every 24" through the foam core to create a patented truss system. The earth sheltered Fellowship Hall is shown on the right side of the Church.

The 100' high water tank towers over the Church. Its 38,000 gallon capacity serves the community of Sparrow Hawk Village from the mountain top. The cross arms are 40' from tip to tip and do not contain water.

The Light of Christ Community Church embraces the daily practice of Christianity as a process of transformation and enlightenment. Promoting the essential Christian principles as set forth in the Holy Bible, the Aquarian Gospel of Jesus the Christ and other sacred scriptures of the world community of religions, we believe in an oral tradition as well as a written, an inner spiritual heritage as well as an outer form.

We recognize in all prophets a harmony, in all scriptures a unity, through all dispensations a continuity. We seek to awaken the Presence within and transform our human nature to live in accord with spiritual law. We embrace that Consciousness Divine which makes all sects, classes, nations and races, one beloved community. Unto this mystical Church and unto its members known and unknown throughout the world, we pledge the allegiance of our hands, hearts and minds.

The teachings of Light of Christ Community Church are eclectic and universalized. We seek to teach, encourage and promote spiritual healing in all its modes and phases. Light of Christ Community Church is an interfaith Christian Church and accepts the teachings of Master Jesus as the Christed One who offers the way to Humanity through the Christian faith.

Interfaith is a group of western and eastern clergy dedicated to bringing people of different faiths together so that we might recognize our common spiritual origin—all people of one God. Each member of the clergy speaks from his particular background, while fully recognizing the validity of other religions and supporting them actively— not simply tolerating but accepting them in truth and love.

Under these principles we are dedicated to the encouragement of individual spiritual growth. Ever present is the appreciation of each life. We salute the "Christ Within" and seek to unfold that consciousness in all its beauty.

TENETS

We believe in One Almighty Power in the Universe, the Cause of all creation.

We believe that in the heart of every living form is found a spark of that Almighty Power.

We believe that each human being can bloom and unfold spiritual potentials and radiate Beauty, Goodness and Truth.

We believe that humanity is guided by Great Ones, who are the Saviors of the world.

We believe that Christ is the vision of perfection. The teachings are the path leading to perfection.

We believe the spirit of each human being is Immortal.

We believe that all humanity is becoming One Family.

We love all religions, traditions, nations and races without discrimination of color, creed or sex.

We believe that each individual must shine personal light and live a life of honesty, nobility, simplicity and justice.

We believe in generosity, in sharing, in giving and receiving in accord with the Laws of Abundance.

We believe that culture and beauty will unite humanity, that a life of sacrificial service reveals and manifests inner divinity. It is only in giving of your life (making sacred) that one truly Becomes.

Light of Christ Community Church

OTHER RELEASES BY
CAROL W. PARRISH-HARRA

Other releases by Carol W. Parrish-Harra include *A New Age Handbook on Death and Dying,* published by DeVorss and Company, Marina del Rey, California in 1982. Suggestions are offered on how to be with a dying person or a bereaved family. The possible occurrence of paranormal events at a near death is acknowledged with a matter-of-factness that will bring comfort and understanding to those unfamiliar with these phenomena. Order from the publisher, or Light of Community Church, P.O. Box 1274, Tahlequah, OK 74465. $5.95 plus $1.00 postage.

Cassette tapes of Carol's classes, lectures and workshops have served as an excellent source of practical guidance for both the curious and the serious. Economically priced, these high quality tapes are offered in handsome albums of 6 tapes each, or sets of 12 C-90 tapes packed in a clear lucite case. A description folder is available on request from: The Village Bookstore, P.O. Box 1274, Tahlequah, OK 74465.